Mim's Story

Christine Ingleton

Mim's Story

Acknowledgements

Thank you Sally, Trish, Steve, Rob, Janet, Judy and Beth for rounding out *Mim's Story* with your own memories, and commenting on early drafts. I feel rich with all that sharing. Thank you to my supporting and challenging readers, Jill, Joelie and Margaret, for suggestions, proofreading and always saying, 'More details, please!'

Mim's Story
ISBN 978 1 76041 029 2
Copyright © Christine Ingleton 2015
Cover photo by Keith Murray, Port Lincoln: Muriel just before her wedding

First published 2015 by
GINNINDERRA PRESS
PO Box 3461 Port Adelaide SA 5015
www.ginninderrapress.com.au

Contents

	Introduction	7
1	A Stepmother's Curses	9
2	Mim's People: the Reads	12
3	Adelaide	25
4	Jim's People: the Ingletons	30
5	Marriage	39
6	Grange	54
7	Hawthorn	75
8	Later years	90
9	Retirement	96
10	Searching for Mim's Father	111

Dedicated to my grandchildren Stevie, Maya, Simone and Eirinn, inheritors of Mim's courage, resilience and love

Introduction

My mother, Henrietta Muriel Read, was born in Broken Hill in 1911. She endured a harsh childhood yet emerged with strength, determination and grace. She didn't know who her father was, she was orphaned at four, brought up by a cruel step-grandmother, and was educated only to grade seven. Yet while she raised her family, she started South Australia's first community kindergarten, became a teacher, pushed against community and medical barriers to intellectual disability, and was a loved 'mother' to many overseas students.

In her twenties, Muriel's friends called her Bunny; her married name was H. Muriel Ingleton; to Dad she was Mu; soon she became my Mum, then to the grandchildren she was Mim. I've used all of these names as the story progresses, but while I always called my parents Mum and Dad, here I call them Mu (later Mim) and Jim. For this picture of her life, I've used family photographs, evidence from Trove, a digitised treasury of old newspapers, and Mim's diaries. The greatest resource has been family life, the stories Mim told and the many conversations her family has shared.

1

A Stepmother's Curses

'I curse you! I curse you! I curse you!' screamed step-grandmother Rose from the front veranda as the dark-haired young woman closed the gate on her childhood at Wilmington. She carried a suitcase, a letter of commendation from the local Methodist minister and her meagre savings. Thin, pinched and frightened, she was barely five feet tall in her size three shoes as she hurried along the main street to catch the train to Adelaide, the journey to her independence. It was 1930, the height of the Great Depression, and my mother was nineteen years old.

I sometimes wonder about the power of those curses, considering the tragedies and obstacles that forged my mother's life and character. But despite being orphaned and enduring a cruel upbringing, she grew up determined to create a family with far more love than she had ever known.

Broken Hill

My mother, Henrietta Muriel Read, was born in Broken Hill on 9 November 1911 to Isobel (or Isabella) Muriel Read. Isobel looks sweet in her photograph, the only one my mother was given, but her childhood was tough. By the time she was ten, Isobel had experienced the deaths of two sisters and a brother, the divorce of her parents and the disappearance of her mother to the Western Australian goldfields.

Isobel was born to Lydia and George Read in Unley in 1888, the second of six children. Following his divorce, Isobel's father was granted custody of his three remaining children: Isobel aged ten, Allan aged eight, and Dorcas aged six. Because his job as a telegrapher was in Port Darwin, George left them in the care of the local church, St Augustine's, Unley, whose minister vouched to the court to have them

Isobel Muriel Read, my grandmother.

My mother Henrietta Muriel Read, aged 4.

looked after. Isobel could hardly have known her father, and now that her mother had left, she was in the hands of strangers. Did she stay with a St Augustine's family? Was she separated from her brother and sister? Did she go to school? Did she work for her living in the house of the St Augustine's family who looked after her?

What we do know is that Isobel moved to Broken Hill, where her uncle and aunt lived, and that her father supported her by paying a monthly allowance of one pound to her landlady. (George mentions this in a diary, but there are no details of his daughter.) We know that at the age of twenty-two Isobel was pregnant, and she was unmarried. Did she dare tell her father she was pregnant? Did her mother ever know? Who was there to help her when she gave birth to my mother, Henrietta Muriel? Above all, who was the father of her child?

To be an unwed mother then was scandalous, especially in a country town, a shame that could not be lived down. But Isobel was fortunate to find a husband to support her and her child. When Muriel was just a year old, at the end of 1912, Isobel married Henry Franklin. The three moved into a neat cottage clad in corrugated iron at 475

475 Beryl Street, Broken Hill.

Beryl Street, Broken Hill, its veranda overlooking the railway line. The cottage is still there today.

Four years later, Isobel became pregnant to Henry. Little Muriel must have been looking forward to having a brother or sister, but now she suffered a tragic double loss. Both the baby and Isobel died in childbirth.

What was Henry to do with four-year-old Henrietta, who was not his child? He sent a telegram to Isobel's father George to inform him of Isobel's death and ask who should care for his granddaughter. The formal photograph of her at this time shows a loved and well cared for child. A young couple came to see Henry and the beautiful little girl, wanting to adopt her. Henrietta liked them but Grandfather decided that she should come to live with him and his wife of six years, Rose. My mother often wondered how different her life would have been if that young couple had adopted her.

At her mother's funeral, Henrietta Muriel felt herself raised up to look into the coffin as she was made to kiss the cold cheek of her mother. That was her earliest memory. The next was being lifted up onto the steam train by her grandfather for the journey to Wilmington, a large town in the lower Flinders Ranges, where she was to spend the rest of her childhood.

2

Mim's People: the Reads

Who was George Amelius Griffiths Read, the man who brought up his granddaughter Muriel, my mother? Born in Australia, his parents were English. His father Robert Read left the army to become a police constable soon after migrating to Australia in 1854. In 1859 Robert married a widow, Mrs Susan Ann Battle (née Hall), at St Luke's Anglican church, Whitmore Square, Adelaide. They had three children – Emily Maud (Em), Herbert and his younger brother George – who all grew up in Mount Barker.

Robert Read's wife, Susan Ann Battle, my great-great-grandmother.

My great-great-grandfather Robert became an inspector of the Mounted Police in Adelaide in early 1867 but due to poor health he resigned from the police force within three years of this promotion. On 1 January 1870, he took a position as Deputy Superintendent of the Fire Brigades at Port Adelaide but by the end of the year, at the age of forty-nine, Robert was dead. Robert, after whom my brother is named, was buried at Mitcham Cemetery, leaving Emily aged nine, Herbert aged seven and George aged five in the care of their mother Susan.

> Mr. Robert Read, who held the appointments of Waterworks Collector and Superintendent of Fire Brigade, Port Adelaide, died suddenly at his residence on Wednesday morning. He had been under the medical care

of Mr. Mortimer, for several days prior to his death, the immediate cause of which was an apoplectic fit. Mr. Read had held various appointments under the Government for many years, and was for a considerable time connected with the mounted police, of which he was a junior inspector. Although he had but a comparatively short residence at the Port, he had earned the respect and good opinions of all with whom he had been brought in contact.

The Register, Thursday, 15 December 1870

My great-grandfather George was well educated according to my mother, but of his childhood I have no record. The story we know begins when he married nineteen-year-old Lydia Simpson at Norwood in 1886. He was twenty-one. Amelia was born that year. Next came my grandmother Isobel, then Allan, Dorcas, Horace and Ada Florence. A handwritten filing card from the Broken Hill Family History Group records the death of the last child, Ada Florence, as published in the Broken Hill newspaper:

Read, Ada Florence May

Sunday a.m. from heat apoplexy, died at residence of Mr Robert Ward, Eyre St SBH.
Dr Horne sent for but died before he arrived. Reported to Coroner.

Barrier Miner 13 February 1899

Ada Florence was four years and three months old when she died. But why was she in a Mr Ward's house in Broken Hill in February 1899? Where were her parents? Her mother Lydia was living in Adelaide while George was working in Darwin. During the three years that George and Lydia were living in different states, their marriage collapsed. Several newspapers of the time tell a vivid story of their divorce in March 1899. Is that why the toddler was in the care of Lydia's older sister Mary Jane? Mary had married Robert Ward in 1886 and they were living in Broken Hill with their seven-year-old son Walter Robert.

Within a month of little Ada Florence's death in Broken Hill, George's petition for divorce on the grounds of his wife's adultery was being heard in an Adelaide court. This was surprising news to me as my mother talked

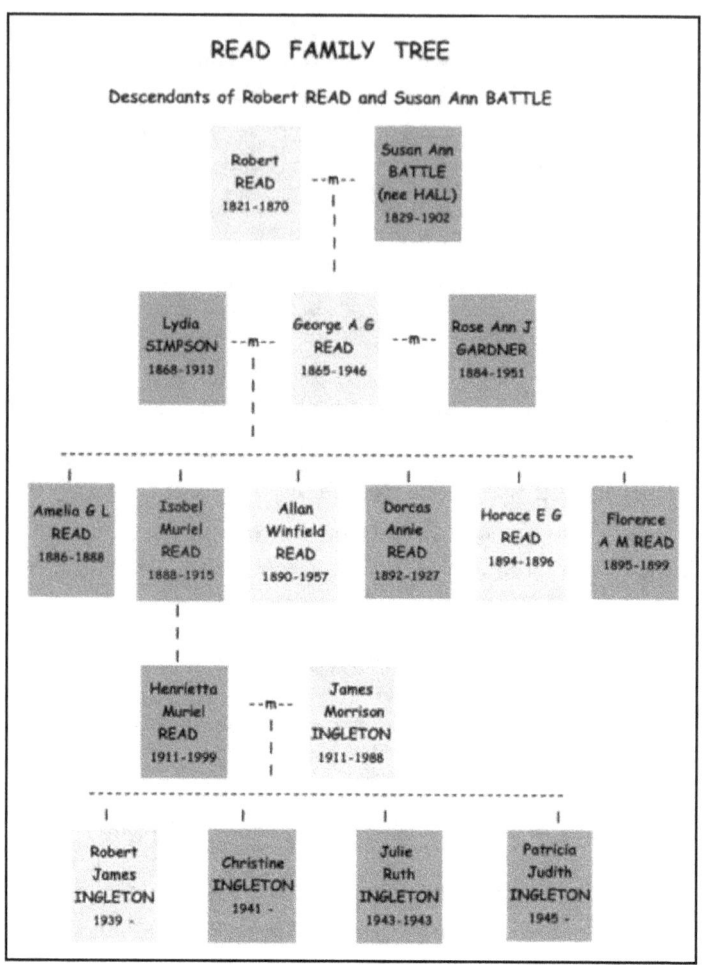

a lot about her grandfather, but she never mentioned that he was divorced. I always understood that George's first wife had died. Perhaps divorce then was as shameful as illegitimacy. This particular divorce was so shameful that several newspapers closely monitored the court proceedings, and Lydia's family literally cut her out of the family Bible!

Divorce

George and Lydia Read had moved to the Northern Territory following George's promotion to the Palmerston telegraph office, near Darwin

Harbour. Here Lydia accused George of violence and drunkenness, while he complained that Lydia 'had a fondness for giving supper parties and neglecting her duties'. Lydia returned to Adelaide with their first child Amelia, later going back to Palmerston after the birth of their second child, Isobel Muriel. Their sons, Allan and Horace, were born in Palmerston, while another daughter, Dorcas, was born in Hotham, Victoria. (Lydia's parents lived in the Ararat/Cathcart region of Victoria so perhaps she went home to them for the birth of the baby.) Although Lydia returned to Palmerston with the children, she disliked the climate and, it seems, her husband as well, and returned to Adelaide permanently.

George supported Lydia and the children with a monthly allowance for the next three years, during which Lydia sent 'loving letters' to him to guarantee her continued income. The allowance came to an abrupt end when George received a letter from a Mrs Foster in Adelaide claiming that Lydia was living with her husband. She demanded that George come to Adelaide immediately to investigate. George arrived to find Lydia living 'in a house which was almost a brothel' with Alfred Foster, with whom she had had a child. George immediately sued for divorce.

The divorce proceedings were reported locally and interstate. On 22 and 23 March 1899 *The South Australian Register* described the sordid events of this marriage. Details also appeared in the *Adelaide Advertiser*, *The Kalgoorlie Miner* and *The West Australian*. Accusations of adultery were aired along with the births of one if not two children who were not George's.

In those days, the act of adultery had to be witnessed in order to be proved, and so various witnesses, some unreliable, were called to give evidence.

A SOUTH AUSTRALIAN DIVORCE SUIT, Adelaide, March 22

If they believed the evidence…no one outside a lunatic asylum would imagine that the respondent [Lydia Read] and co-respondent [Foster] had not committed adultery. The evidence of Mrs Monaghan [a witness], a drunken woman, who showed little sense of propriety, the manner in which Mrs. Read and Foster lived in the same house and all the subsequent circumstances induced [the judge] to believe that they committed adultery. He thought the case was proved up to the hilt.

The West Australian, 23 March 1899

At the Supreme Court to-day before Chief Justice Way, G.A.G. Read, a telegraph operator stationed at Port Darwin sued for divorce from his wife, Lydia Read, on the grounds of adultery with Alfred Foster and others unknown. It was shown that Mrs. Read gave birth to a child and that she and Foster had lived as man and wife. His Honour said that it had been proved beyond a doubt that adultery had been committed by some person unknown nine months before the birth of the child.

The Advertiser, 23 March 1899

Lydia claimed that the birth of her fifth child, Ada Florence, 'was a cross one [a breach birth], owing to ill-treatment' by her husband. Under cross-examination, George's defence included,

> Occasionally took too much drink. Never took drink into the bedroom. Never got under the bed to drink it. Do not remember taking carbolic acid. Never took poison. Would not say he was not drunk on Christmas Eve, 1893. Would not say he did not take poison then. Had no recollection of it. Would deny that he threatened to cut his wife's throat with a razor. A man when drunk might say anything. Never threatened to shoot his wife with a double-barrelled gun. Did not do it when he was drunk. Did not hit his wife the Sunday before the fifth child was born. Had no recollection of ever having done so. Remembered being locked up. Did not know who gave him in charge. It was best known to his wife. When he was locked up the case was dismissed. Might have given his wife a 'good talking to' and a 'box on the ears,' but did not call that ill-treatment. She went away the last time by mutual consent. Did not like her to go but he agreed because it was better for her health and the education of the children. That was in April, 1896. Was sober when his wife left Port Darwin, and did not swear at her at she left the wharf.

The case continued:

In April 1895 [Lydia] left Palmerston taking the children with her. In October 1896 she wrote to her husband telling him not to let his family know where she was living and counsel stated he would prove that while in Adelaide she was 'carrying on' with Alfred Foster and was living in a house which was almost a brothel. In August 1898 she gave birth to a child. All this time the husband was receiving affectionate letters from his wife and he sent her money. His suspicions were aroused by information from Adelaide, and he made enquiries.

Lydia Read, the respondent, said she met Foster first in the beginning of May 1898. He lodged in the same house and her brother stayed in the house at the same time… She claimed she never occupied a bed with Foster and her daughter [Isobel] Muriel.

South Australian Register, 22 March 1899

I found that last statement most upsetting, knowing that ten-year-old Isobel was witnessing all that went on in that house. No wonder the youngest child was sent to stay with her aunt and uncle in Broken Hill, while Isobel, Allan and Dorcas were soon put into the care of St Augustine's parish, Unley.

As I write this, I'm looking at the Simpson family Bible that has just come to light. An unexpected phone call came from Allan's grandson with the following message: 'I'm Allan Read and I believe we are related. I have some information for you and hope I can meet you this morning!' I met with Allan and his wife Helen, and my brother Robert and his wife Janet, that morning – he is the first relative of our mother's we have ever met.

Allan had inherited the family Bible with the story that his great-

Allan Read, Chris and Rob.

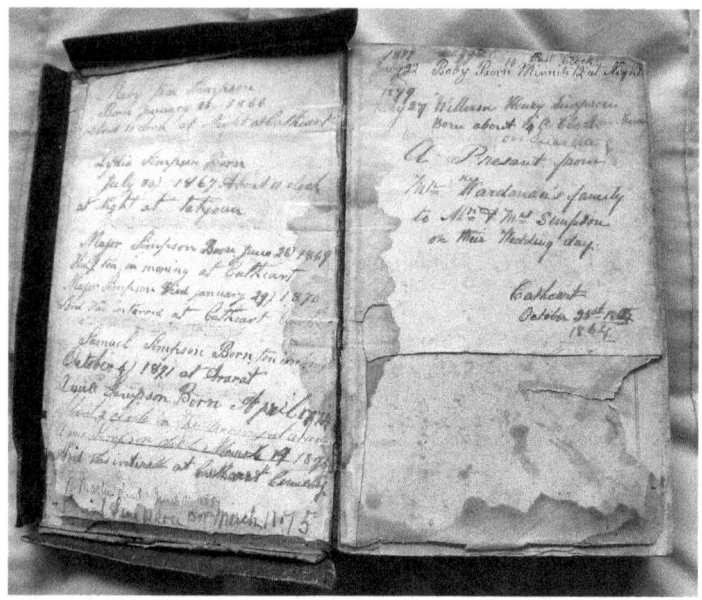

Bible with page cut.

grandmother Lydia Simpson had been physically cut out of the records in the front pages, but he didn't know why. Now he knows why the family disowned her, and now I understand why Rose so bitterly cursed my mother twenty years later: 'Out of the gutter you came, and back to the gutter you'll go!'

The Bible was published in 1863. On the first page is an inscription to Lydia's parents:

> A Presant from
> Mr Wardsmans' family
> to Mr and Mrs Simpson
> on their Wedding day.
> Cathcart
> October 25th 1864

Inside the front cover, the Simpson children's births are recorded, beginning with Mary Jane in 1866, followed by Lydia, Major, Samuel and Annie. Turning the cut page, we can see at the top, 'Florence Rose-May, Simpson, Baby Born half past One afternoon May 9 1885'. Is

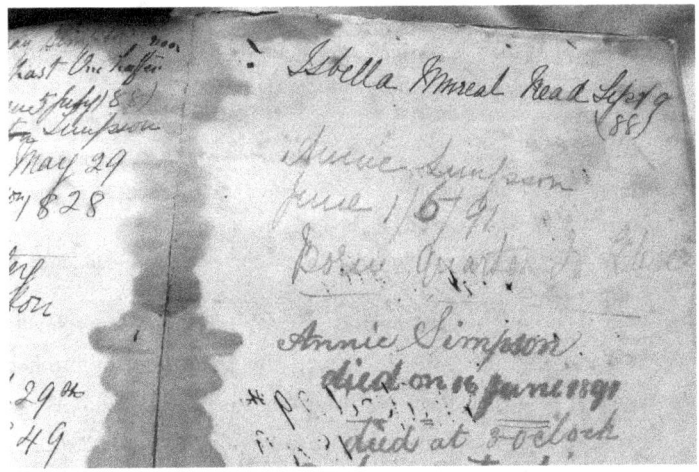
Bible page 3.

this Florence Ada May Read? On the next page, in a different hand, is my grandmother's name, 'Isbella Mureal Read Sept 9 (88)', but it is not linked to her parents.

On the fourth page is an inscription to the firstborn of the next generation, Mary Jane Simpson, Lydia's older sister, on her marriage to Robert Ward. There is only one other reference to any of Lydia's children, and that is on the back page where Grandfather Samuel Simpson's death at seventy-eight is recorded, and another hand has written, 'Dorcas Read, granddaughter of above'. Perhaps Dorcas had stayed with her extended family in Victoria and been loved by her maternal grandfather.

The Overland Telegraph

Following the divorce George returned to work at Palmerston. In 1902 he moved to Daly Waters, where for the next seven years he was in charge of the Daly Waters repeater station on the famous Overland Telegraph line.

> In 1870 the South Australian government…agreed to build a 3,200 kilometre overland telegraph line connecting Darwin with Port Augusta, if the British-Australian Telegraph Company would lay a submarine cable from Java to Darwin. When completed in 1872 Australia could speak with the rest of the world.

Connecting Adelaide and the rest of Australia, through Darwin, with England by means of a single wire in 1872, was one of the greatest engineering achievements of the nineteenth century.

As many as eleven repeater stations were built along the Overland Telegraph Line between Port Augusta and Darwin which was completed in August 1872. Using the morse key, operators at the stations were able to communicate with the world 24 hours a day.

http://www.southaustralianhistory.com.au/overland.htm

While working on the Overland Telegraph, George kept a small, tan, leather-bound diary which has been transcribed by my brother Rob and can be read at http://www.territorystories.nt.gov.au. George records rather dryly facts from his life as a supervisor and quartermaster for the gangs in his section. He was responsible for maintaining the repeater stations on the line from Katherine in the north to Tennant Creek in the south, a distance of almost seven hundred kilometres by road today. George travelled back and forth on horseback between the railway settlements with supplies, camping out whenever he was on the move, tracking purchases, stores and livestock, and checking the state of the wells. We can hear George's voice in this diary excerpt:

"On monday evening **10th Nov 1902** left DW* for No 3 Well with 123 cattle and 3 black boys. Came across McNamara about 8 miles out with a broken shaft, having gone against a stump in road, arrived at No 3 Well 9.45a 12th Wednesday. Dropped on road 4 small cows & 6 calves which were too low in condition to travel the long dry stage at this time of the year - for no tucker - run out.
Daly Waters

Thursday 13th 1902
Tally   Cattle 100 Lost 13 & 10
         Goats 129 do 27
         Horses 29 do 4

Much later, George told his granddaughter Muriel that one day, riding alone in the desert, he had a bad fall from his horse, losing two of his upper front teeth. Unconscious, he was discovered by Aboriginal men whose own initiation rites had included the knocking out of the two top front teeth. Seeing George's teeth, they accepted him as if he were an initiated man and cared for him. My brother now has the waddy they gave him, which has been kept ever since as a threat against intruders! A lasting legacy for our family has been my great-grandfather's respect for Aboriginal people, passed down to us through my mother.

From 1909, George worked as a relieving postmaster, travelling all over South Australia to manage rural post offices. It was 1915 when he arrived from the remote town of Oodnadatta to attend his daughter Isobel Muriel's funeral in Broken Hill. Then with his orphaned granddaughter, he took the new steam train to Wilmington, where he was postmaster. Waiting for him there was Rose-Ann (née Gardner), his second wife, whom he had married in May 1909 at Hindmarsh. She was almost twenty years his junior and their marriage produced no children, but now, with the death of George's fourth child, Rose suddenly became 'Grandma' to this little girl, four-year-old Henrietta Muriel. The Wilmington post office with its attached house became Muriel's home for the next fifteen years.

Wilmington

Rose was angry. She resented having this child foisted on her. Rose's life had been hard, with little schooling. At sixteen she had found herself pregnant and had been forced to give up her baby for adoption. Probably she had not been allowed to see her newborn before it was taken away. Now she was saddled with another shameful woman's illegitimate child. She never let Muriel forget the unfairness of that. 'From the gutter you came, and to the gutter you will go!' was her refrain. Rose frequently taunted the small child with the stigma of being a bastard. She abused her mentally and physically until the day she hurled those final curses from the veranda, the day Muriel escaped.

Wilmington Post Office and house, about 1925.

My mother's childhood with Rose was lonely and unhappy. No child was allowed to come into the house to play after school, nor was Muriel allowed to play at anyone else's house. Sundays were for going to Sunday school and Bible reading only. No games and no outside playing were allowed. One of Muriel's consolations was the family cat. One Sunday, Rose caught Muriel curiously peering under the cat's tail, and thrashed her for playing with the cat on a Sunday. No one saw the welts from her step-grandmother's thrashings, or the daily beltings for jobs imperfectly done or for being a minute late home from school. No one knew about the terrible kick in the genitals when the nine-year-old was kneeling down cleaning the fireplace one morning, or the beatings between her legs with a poker where no one would see the bruises. No one heard the threats that if she misbehaved she would be sent away as a ward of the state to labour on a farm.

As she grew older, Muriel was aware that the townspeople knew she was being abused. How much was her grandfather aware of? When she talked about him, my mother always spoke warmly of her grandfather. She felt loved by him but was certainly not well protected by him. Was Muriel too fearful to tell him what Rose did to her? Did he have no idea? Everyone knew the postmaster and his family and there may have been gossip, but in this country town there was no rescue from her abuse.

Reluctance to interfere was not unusual in country towns and

Rose, George and Muriel at Wilmington with Mr and Mrs Slee, about 1925.

Wilmington was no different. Originally known as Beautiful Valley, the town was settled in the 1860s, becoming a busy centre for several outlying farming districts. By the late 1890s, along the wide, tree-lined main street there were three hotels, a flour mill, a butter factory that exported Beau-Val butter to England, a large general store and several smaller shops. When the railway reached Wilmington in 1915, the year George brought Muriel from Broken Hill, the town served as the railhead for sheep and grain, and became renowned for an award-winning Challenge Stripper and stump-jump plough designed and engineered there.

Wilmington had a three-roomed primary school built of stone. Each room of twenty square feet was bursting with about thirty-five children. Muriel was a model student, top of the class in spelling, reading and

Wilmington Primary School: Muriel second row, fifth from left.

Muriel at Wilmington Railway Station.

writing. A class photo shows a thin, serious child, long dark hair parted severely in the middle, one of the smallest children in her row.

In 1923 Muriel passed the Grade Seven Qualifying Certificate and left school. She had just turned twelve. Now she worked at home and helped her grandfather at the post office. There was no question of her continuing her education. Only wealthy families could afford to send their children to Adelaide for secondary education, and even then only the sons were sent.

The Wilmington post office had opened in 1878 with daily mail services, and shortly afterwards a Savings Bank of SA agency was established there too. It was 1914 when the first telephone exchange in the district opened with ten subscribers. In her teens, Muriel became the switchboard operator at the post office, her clear, soft voice familiar to those locals sharing a party line to their homes. With their bakelite handsets mounted high on the wall, callers standing to use the phone could easily listen in to the conversations of the other households on the same line – a good reason for being careful about what went on in the privacy of one's own home!

3

Adelaide

By the time Muriel gathered the courage to leave Wilmington, she was an experienced telephonist. Stepping off the train at the Adelaide railway station in 1930, she was met by Reverend George W. Shapley MBE, who had been the Methodist minister in Wilmington for the preceding five years. He knew the Reads and their bright granddaughter well, for Muriel had been a prize-winner for learning all the books of the Bible by heart, and a Sunday school teacher. The Shapley family took her into their home, where she was warmly embraced by the Reverend George's wife and their two daughters. The girls played tennis, went for picnics, swam, entertained friends (without a drop of alcohol, being Methodists), and often went to Port Lincoln on family holidays.

My mother stopped using the hated name Henrietta, reducing it to H. in front of her second name, Muriel, while her friends gave her the nickname Bunny, which stayed for the next fifty years. She was Muriel at work and Bunny at play. And play she did! She was a daredevil, enjoying riding Keith Murray's Harley-Davidson at Port Lincoln, and she was thrilled to celebrate her seventieth birthday with a ride on a Harley. In her forties, she wore my school uniform to a fancy dress party and was reprimanded for being seen smoking in uniform! At Port Lincoln, the Murrays – Keith, Peg, Don and Jean – became Bunny's lifelong friends, later moving to Adelaide with Peg's mother. Jean, though born with severe cerebral palsy, lived to an old age, the longest-term resident of the Julia Farr Centre. Peg's mother's hundred-year-old couch graced our family living room.

Muriel arrived in Adelaide at the height of the 1929–32 Great Depression. In mid-1930 the unemployment rate was 21% and by

Bunny on Keith Murray's motorbike.

mid-1932 almost 32%. At nineteen, she must have had excellent references and presentation to secure her first job on the switchboard at J.N. Taylor & Co. Ltd, manchester warehousemen and general merchants, in Grenfell Street. There she met Nell, the boss's daughter, who was attending Adelaide University part-time. They became lifelong friends, as have her daughter Beverley and I. Now that she was working, Muriel supported herself and lived in a boarding house in the city. She revelled in her independence and social life, and enjoyed her job as a telephonist. The cruelty of her childhood seemed far behind.

One day, the past thundered into her new life. It was morning tea break at work. A switchboard operator had taken a call from a man who wanted this message to be passed to Muriel: 'If you would like to contact your father, please ring [this number] tonight; I am only in town tonight.' Muriel was shocked. 'Your father'? Who was her father? Why was he contacting her now? What did he want? She was panic-stricken. What should she do? Should she ring? Did she have the courage to ring? Who would answer? What would she say? The day passed in agony. She didn't know what to do. She went home to the boarding house, nervous, scared and unable to speak to anyone, not even to her best friend Maisie, whose room was down the corridor. The evening passed in sickening indecision. Until it was too late to ring.

For the rest of her life, Muriel regretted not having made that phone call. She missed her only chance. Who was her father? She never found out. Not until after her death at eighty-seven were clues discovered in a history centre at Broken Hill. But now, in her early twenties, she felt confused and alone.

Harry Hughes

It was 1934. Bunny was in love with Harry Hughes, a handsome, dark-haired mechanic, just a few months her senior. His parents George and Edie Hughes loved this petite, polite, gentle young woman and came to look on her as a daughter, just as she looked on them as the parents she had never had. George Hughes was chief accountant of the Executor Trustee and Agency Co. He and Edie were delighted when Harry proposed, and they gave the young couple their warmest support.

Harry Hughes.

Harry and Bunny went shopping in Hindmarsh Square for a beautiful glory box, a large brocade-covered chest, its top generously padded, making a perfect seat for a bay window. (My daughter Sally has that glory box today, a reminder of the happiest days of Bunny's life.) But in a short time Bunny and the Hughes family were bound in a terrible tragedy.

Coming home from the city on Saturday evening, 5 October 1935, Harry and Bunny were on a drop-centre tram as it rattled through the parklands. Harry was standing smoking with other men in the open drop-centre while Bunny sat on a bench inside the enclosed compartment. Harry casually leaned out the open doorway. Just then the tram swayed. There was a shocking thud against a tram pole. The tram juddered to a stop. In the silence Bunny heard blood spattering on the wooden floor, the splash of each drop never forgotten. Harry lay motionless, bleeding profusely from the head. The men surrounded him, preventing Bunny from getting too close.

'It's all right, love. It's only a blood nose,' said someone.

Another passed her a lighted cigarette. 'Here, you better have this, love.'

An ambulance rushed Harry to the Royal Adelaide Hospital. When Bunny ran in to Emergency, she cried out to the nurse, 'Where's Harry? Is he all right?'

The nurse stared at her. 'He's dead of course.'

The accident was reported in newspapers in all Australian states; an inquest was held on 23 October, 1935. One of the reports read,

MAN KILLED ON TRAM
Fiancee Was a Passenger
ADELAIDE, Sunday.

Harry Allan Hughes, aged 24 years, of Romford street, West Hindmarsh, was standing in the gangway of a moving tram in which his fiancee was seated, when his head struck a tramway standard, fracturing his skull. He died half an hour later in the Adelaide Hospital.

The Argus, Melbourne, Monday 7 October 1935

Bunny went to bed at nights hoping she would never wake up.

Following the tragedy, she continued to work on the switchboard at J.N. Taylor's with her beautiful speaking voice and impeccable telephone manner. Mr Cliff Cornell, managing director of Cornell Ltd, was so impressed by her when she transferred him to Mr Taylor that he asked her to work for him. Cornell's was a large importer and wholesaler of cigarettes, cycle and car parts, fancy goods and, later, of whitegoods. Its sister company Lenroc's (Cornell spelt backwards), specialised in motorbikes and pushbikes. It didn't take long for Mr Cliff to poach Miss Read from J.N. Taylor's by offering her a higher wage to join his business just around the corner in Hyde Street.

Thrilled with the rise, Muriel accepted. Over fifty-five employees worked at Cornell's, including the much-loved nightwatchman Mr Bill (Walkie) Walker. During the Depression, most of Cornell's staff retained their employment due to the company's strategy of every worker reducing their hours to save their colleagues' jobs. There were strong bonds between staff. Years later, when we were aged seven and nine, one of the Cornell sons, David (Cornie Cornflakes to us!), gave Robert and me the most wonderful Christmas presents: our first bicycles.

Drop-centre tram.

4

Jim's People: the Ingletons

In 1936, Muriel settled in to work at the much larger switchboard and was quietly admired by a young employee, Jim Ingleton. Jim had started work at Cornell's as an errand boy just after his fourteenth birthday in January 1925. Now he had a responsible desk job in the tobacco and fancy goods department on the ground floor. At the desk alongside him sat his young sister Beth. They worked under the watchful eye of the director, Mr Len Cornell, who could observe everyone from his glassed-walled office.

One day, Mr Len came to Beth and quietly asked if she would mind moving to the switchboard to replace Muriel. He wanted Muriel to become his secretary. Beth, who did not like one of the employees who sat near her desk, readily agreed to the move. Now Muriel, promoted to personal secretary, was working alongside Jim, much to his pleasure. Little did Jim know then that some twenty years later he would become a director of Cornell Ltd on Mr Cliff's death.

As Jim was to become my father, his Scottish history comes into the picture. Jim was born James Morrison Ingleton, named after his mother's father. The name James goes a long way back in the Ingleton family, and has come forward through my brother Robert James to his son David James, through Robert's daughter Susie to Phillip James, and through me to my son Stephen James Thomas.

From at least 1739, generations of Ingletons lived in Kirkintilloch, Dunbarton, Scotland. Jim's grandfather Ralph Wardlaw Ingleton (senior), happened to be born in Lancashire in 1859, but by the age of twelve he was living in Glasgow in a crowded household. Ralph's father, however, was living elsewhere in Glasgow. Glasgow was a highly industrialised city then, and living conditions for workers were dire. An excerpt from Wikipedia describes Glasgow as a city of contrasts:

> Between 1870 and 1914, Glasgow ranked as one of the richest and finest cities in Europe. On the other hand, however, the city suffered from appalling social problems of poverty, crime and disease. The massively unequal distribution of wealth meant that the splendid mansions in the West End were a marked contrast to the wynds and closes of the High Street, Saltmarket and Gallowgate areas in the East End. There were serious typhus epidemics in 1837 and 1847 and the first cholera outbreak in Scotland in 1832 killed 10,000 people. Between the 1830s and the late 1850s, death rates in the cities rose to peaks not seen since the 17th century.
> www.bbc.co.uk/history/scottishhistory/
> victorian/trails_victorian_glasgow.shtml

By the time he was twelve, Jim's grandfather Ralph was working as a message boy. In his teens, Ralph became a plasterer and at nineteen he married a young Glasgwegian woman, Jane Morrison, also nineteen. Their marriage was on 17 June 1879 and their first child Janet was born seven weeks later. By the time their second child James was born, Ralph and Jane were anxious to get away from their grim life in Glasgow. Janet was four and baby James, Jim's father, was almost two when the family made their way to Plymouth to join the 405 government immigrants for the ten-week voyage to Australia on the ship *The Aldergrove*. The Ingletons arrived at Port Adelaide on

The Aldergrove (courtesy http://digital.slv.vic.gov.au)

31 October 1883. They were among the 'qualified emigrants who received passage money or land grants in the destination country as an alternative to receiving poor relief' (http://familysearch.org/learn/wiki/en/Scotland_Emigration_and_Immigration).

The family settled in Stepney, where seven more children were born. Four of the girls, including twins, died of whooping cough before the age of two. My great-grandmother Jane lived to the age of

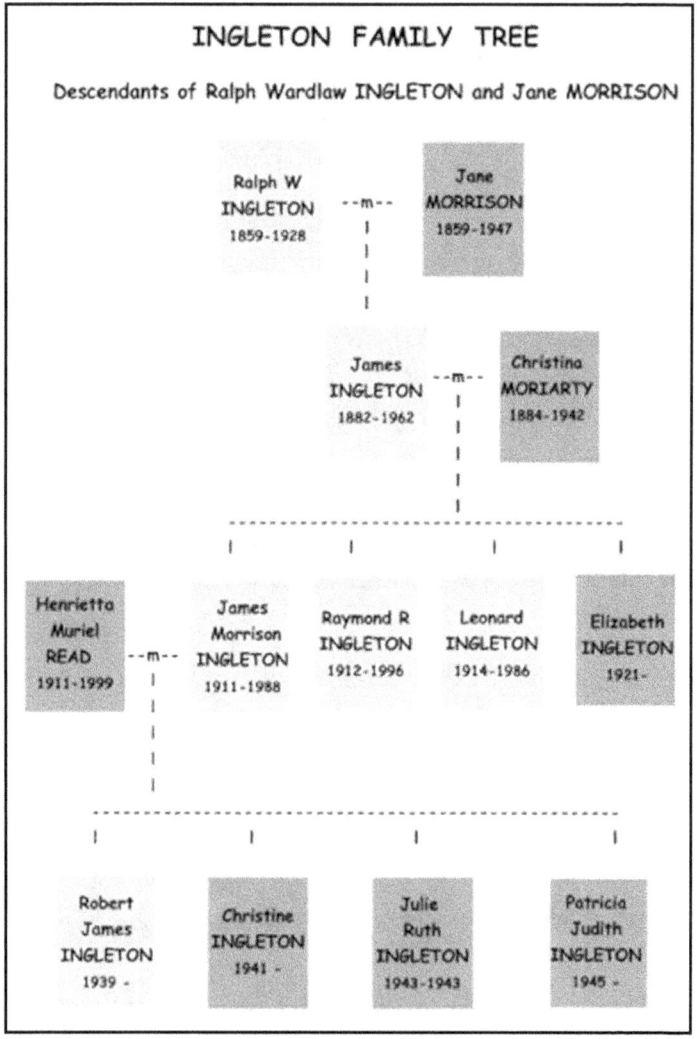

eighty-eight, remembered fondly by my mother for her warmth and her strong Scottish accent.

My father Jim was reluctant to talk about or delve into the unhappy history with his father, Grandpa James. This became clear to me one night at home with Mim and Jim at Sussex Terrace. The phone rang; someone was researching the Ingleton family tree and asked if Jim could help with information. He refused outright, and that was that. We do know that Grandpa James enlisted at the age of nineteen to fight in the Boer War in 1901–2 with the 6th South Australian Imperial Bushmen Contingent. On returning to Adelaide, he became apprenticed as a fitter and turner and in 1910 he married Christina (Teen) Mary Moriarty, widow of Mr Bill Bennett. Teen was born in Norwood and had two brothers, Fred and Will, who supported her during the hard years of her marriage to Grandpa James.

Grandpa James's carpentry was well regarded. One claim to fame is his work on the installation of the grand staircase at the Hayward mansion at Carrick Hill in the late 1930s. The Haywards had imported much of the sixteenth, seventeenth and eighteenth century panelling, staircases, doors and windows from the demolition sale of Beaudesert, a Tudor mansion in Staffordshire, England. They imported and decorated each room with beautiful William Morris wallpapers. After their death, the mansion with its historic staircase was given to the state in 1983 and is now open to the public.

With a friend, Grandpa James built his family's home in 1921, a bungalow that still stands at 37 Collingrove Avenue, Broadview. The generous block had fruit trees and vegetable gardens out the back and flowers at the front. The home had only two bedrooms, so Grandpa's three sons Jim, Ray and Len slept in the enclosed veranda, while Beth, born ten years after Len, slept inside. Family and social life centred on the enormous dining room, twice the size of the sitting room that was kept as a formal room for visitors.

The four children were brought up with plenty of open space. Beth kept her pet kangaroo on vacant land opposite (now a bowling green)

Chris, Beth and Rob at 37 Collingrove Avenue, Broadview.

until the 'roo grew too big to contain. Beth was still living at home with her mother when Teen died suddenly in 1942. I was only one year old at the time and have no memory of the grandmother I was named after. Stephen's daughter, Simone Christine, has her name as well.

Now, as I write, Beth is a very active ninety-three, and there's a wonderful story to tell. At the gym a few weeks ago she was chatting to a ninety-three-year-old man who was very excited about the new car he'd just bought.

Beth said, 'You're lucky! I'm not allowed to have one!'

'What do you mean, you're not allowed?'

'When I told my girls I wanted to buy a new car to celebrate my ninetieth they said, "Oh, Mum, it's not worth it at this age!"'

Len, Jim, Beth and Ray Ingleton.

Rob, Chris, Judy, Janet and Beth, celebrating Beth's ninetieth birthday.

Beth went home and related this conversation to her daughters. They were embarrassed that they'd stopped her from buying something she really wanted, so they told her to go ahead and buy a new car. A few days later, my cousin Jill, Beth's eldest daughter, went with her to test drive a Toyota Yaris. The next day, Beth tried three more cars, this time alone, and the same day bought a new Barina Spark with Bluetooth and iPod connectivity.

'Yes!' she exclaimed. 'It's got all the bells and whistles. I'll get to know them in time!'

I don't know where Grandpa James went to school, but it is said that his younger brother Ralph (junior) ran away from Prince Alfred College to Perth, where he put his age up to enlist in the army and sailed off to war. He was only fifteen.

Grandpa James sent his three sons to Sturt Street Primary School in the city, where my father Jim, the eldest son, sat in the same class as the famous ballet dancer Sir Robert Helpmann. Jim was bright and wanted to be a draughtsman. At the end of Year Seven he won a place at the Tech, a non-government school originally located on the top floor of the Brookman Building, then part of the School of Mines. (In the 1970s, Adelaide Tech became Glenunga High, and later the Brookman Building became part of UniSA.) Adelaide Tech was a selective school created originally to improve the educational standard of young men who planned to study at the School of Mines and Industries… Partly because of accommodation constraints and partly to maintain academic excellence, entry was restricted to high achievement in the Qualifying Certificate at the end of primary school or to an Entrance Examination. At times as many potential students were denied entry as were successful in doing so. For most of its history the course was basically for three years with the Intermediate Examination being attempted after two years and the Leaving Examination after three years.

Old Scholars website

My father Jim had just turned twelve when he started at the Tech and was not quite fourteen when he gained his Intermediate Certificate, including Dimensional Sketching and Lettering and Showcard Writing, taken at the School of Mines.

Jim's younger brothers, Ray and Len, went to Adelaide High School. Ray went on to the School of Mines to qualify as an accountant and later married Nell. They had one child, Peter. His youngest brother Len, unable to stand his father, completed his Intermediate and at the age of sixteen left for Sydney. There he prospered in the wholesale jewellery trade with his agency Lustre, and in property, eventually becoming a charming millionaire, the first and only in his family. As children, we enjoyed Uncle Len's cheeriness, fun and generosity, just as Sally remembers him as a child, along with his gifts of exotic overseas stamps. His beloved wife, Bess, died of cancer and they had no children. Later he married his secretary, Glad. Unfortunately, alcohol was one of his problems. Beth, the youngest sibling by ten years, attended Adelaide Girls High School, later marrying Ralph Fairweather and having four daughters, Jill, Anne, Sally and Lynne.

On his fourteenth birthday in January 1925, Jim went to work to support his family. His father was frequently away and did not provide for them. Beth, recalling the events at ninety-three, says she was not privy to the whispered conversations between her mother and older brothers concerning the long absences of their father. From behind closed doors, however, she understood that her father was living with his mistress in Perth. The sons were angry, while Teen managed as best she could with the support of her children and her two brothers.

YMCA

In his teens and early twenties, Jim was active in the Young Men's Christian Association (YMCA) where he excelled in leadership and in a wide range of sports and skills. Each of the Ingleton brothers was in turn president of the Boys' Cabinet of the YMCA: Jim in 1928, Ray in 1929 and Len in 1930. A photo of all three celebrated this under the caption 'Brother succeeds Brothers' in *The News* on 30 July 1930. Jim was vice captain of the YMCA Kia-Ora Cricket Club 1928–9, as well as a keen basketballer, and he earned several certificates of merit at the annual YMCA carnivals. These certificates show a surprising range of talents. In 1927, when he was sixteen, Jim came first in Bible reading and sermonette, and gained highest points in the religion section; he was second in woodwind solo, potato race and religious essay, and third in hop, step and jump, humorous song, impromptu speech and Bible recital. In 1930 he won similar awards with the addition of pingpong, relay race, volleyball and basketball! Later, Jim was a champion ballroom dancer, dressing impeccably for dancing competitions. His success, however, brought him into direct conflict with his role as a lay preacher at Pirie Street Methodist Church.

'Jim,' admonished the minister, 'it's either ballroom dancing or the church. You can't have both! You'll have to make a choice.'

Jim scarcely hesitated. He gave away his church allegiance altogether, instead maintaining through the YMCA his strong values, community spirit and ethic for social responsibility.

Jim was part of a sturdy support network, which at one time raised money to enable one of the YMCA boys, John Rayment, a musician, to have an operation to correct his severely crossed eyes. John was one of Jim's best friends, and was later groomsman at Jim and Muriel's wedding, with his wife Jean as a bridesmaid. The YMCA boys stood by John years later when, one day in January 1952, his wife and three children went missing. The police found her car at Semaphore. Jean had taken the children aged five, two and ten months out of the car, walked across the sand and waded into the sea with them until they drowned. Then she drowned herself. I can still see the children's upstairs room, on a visit months afterwards, with beds, clothes and toys left just as they had been on that shocking day.

In his youth, despite his confident presentation, Jim was a little shy, and had worked hard to overcome a stammer. Now he was in love with Muriel. He had known Harry Hughes and socialised with the young couple, after Harry's death promising Muriel he would watch out for her. Two years later, he wanted to invite Muriel out but it was too soon for her to want to be with another man. She could not let go of the loss of the intense happiness of being in love, of the idea of her life with Harry, that ideal time of being loved unconditionally. Muriel had not come to terms with the shock and grief that had so shattered her life. But Jim persisted, even flying on more than one occasion in a very small plane to Port Lincoln, where she went on holidays with the Shapleys to get over Harry's death.

5

Marriage

Jim proposed to Muriel with an engagement ring bearing a large yellow diamond set on an ornate shoulder of tiny diamond chips. Inside the gold wedding band is still the engraving: Mu–Jim 9.7.38. She liked him very much but she confided in me that she was never in love with him – she felt she could never be in love again. They married in a packed Pirie Street Methodist Church on 9 July 1938.

READ–INGLETON

> The marriage of Muriel Read, granddaughter of Mr and Mrs G. Read of North Walkerville, to James Morrison, eldest son of Mr and Mrs J. Ingleton, of 37 Collingrove Avenue, Broadview, will be solemnised at the Pirie St Methodist Church on Saturday, the 9th July at 7pm. All friends and relatives are cordially invited to ceremony. No reception.
>
> *The Advertiser*, Saturday 2 July 1938

Muriel, who was always Mu to Jim, wore a traditional long-sleeved white gown with a swirling train and veil, carried a classic bouquet, and was attended by two bridesmaids in dark red velvet, Maisie Lean (later Bevan) and Jean Rayment, with two groomsmen, John Rayment and Jim's brother Len. The photos portray a lavish wedding party. I wonder if Mu's grandfather and stepmother Rose were there, as it was a family friend, Jim Claridge (founder of Claridge Motors), who gave her away.

Jim and Mu rented their first home at Millswood. But six months later, when they were both at work, a fire destroyed most of their wedding gifts.

Mu and Jim's wedding, 9 July 1938; Jean Rayment and Maisie Bevan on left, Len Ingleton and John Rayment on right.

Millswood fire

Millswood Estate Fire. At 12.13pm yesterday, the Unley Fire Brigade received a call to a fire at the house occupied by Mr. J.M. Ingleton of Millswood Crescent, Millswood Estate. Two appliances were sent from Adelaide, but the Unley Brigade had the fire under control in 10 minutes. A room and a passage and their contents were damaged, but the rest of the house was saved.

The Advertiser, Thursday 5 January 1939

On the footpath outside the scene they were befriended by a young couple living nearby, Ron and Flo Close. Ron and Flo offered accommodation for them until they could find another place. That friendship continued for over fifty years, with many a family visit to the Closes at Marryatville, where the kids, four of them and three of us, climbed through the back fence and played along the creek that now runs through the grounds of Marryatville High School.

9 Railway Terrace, Edwardstown, 2014.

Mu and Jim soon moved into their own home at 9 Railway Terrace, Edwardstown, with its veranda of three arches, a backyard of lawn, Hills hoist, fruit trees and vegetable garden surrounded by corrugated iron fencing. Railway Terrace was lined with huge old pine trees, as it is today, their roots and debris roughening the footpaths, with aniseed bushes big enough to hide in lining the railway tracks across the road.

Family

It was 1939. Their first baby was on the way and World War II was about to be unleashed. Mu's first pregnancy was unremarkable but six weeks before the baby was due her waters broke, and she was rushed to Memorial Hospital. She laboured for three agonising days until it seemed she would not survive. A minister was called to give her the last rites. But then Robert James was born on 15 August, in what was then called a 'dry birth'. The birth notice said, 'Strictly no visitors.' Robert was premature, underweight and had difficulty feeding. Back home, breastfeeding became extremely painful and the local GP was called on three occasions. He finally diagnosed Mu's many breast lumps as cancer and sent her to hospital with the baby, for a mastectomy. The nuns at Calvary told her how thrilled they were to have a baby in the ward! The surgeon's cut revealed a breast filled with abscesses, a finding

Robert, five and a half months.

that also revealed a shockingly incompetent GP. Jim was set to sue him when all medical fees were hastily waived. His opinion of the medical profession was soured.

As baby Robert grew, Mu looked for information on how to care for babies, having had no experience and missing a mother to guide her. She wanted her children to feel loved and to be well cared for, determined that her own childhood experience would never be repeated. She welcomed the support of the Mothers and Babies Health Association, the MBHA. Her excellent mother care was rewarded when beautiful baby Robert won a baby competition at nine months old! How did he win 2,813 votes, seventy years before Facebook was born?

Marion and Black Forest MBHA

> Lady Mawson, vice-president of the central executive or the MBHA. announced the winners of a popular baby competition at a children's frolic in the Presbyterian Church hall, Black Forest, on Saturday afternoon… The competition was won by Robert Ingleton with 2,813 votes. Peter Mayne gained second place with 1,566 votes.
>
> *The Advertiser*, Monday 20 May 1940

In those days, the latest baby care regime advised regular-as-clockwork feeding and sleeping, and no picking up of crying babies for fear of spoiling them. Dr Truby King, a New Zealand surgeon with an interest in child development, nutrition and psychology, was the leading exponent of childcare in Australia in that era. He championed breastfeeding during the first twelve to eighteen months, and believed it was character-building not to cuddle infants. The regular routine appealed to Mu but not the harshness of denying physical contact. Much earlier in his career, in another area of expertise, Dr King had been challenged by the physician Agnes Elizabeth Lloyd Bennett when she 'publicly opposed his stance that higher education for women was detrimental to their maternal functions and hence to the human race' (Bennett, Agnes Elizabeth Lloyd (1872–1960), *Australian Dictionary of Biography*). That view was widespread in my mother's lifetime!

One day, Mu saw an advertisement for a lecture by Mrs Sadie Crawford, a young mother and wife of the Rev. Norman Crawford, a practising psychologist and Anglican priest. At the lecture, Sadie preached a gospel of bringing up babies with love and security, and Mu was very impressed. Wanting to learn more, she spoke to Sadie after the meeting and so began a long and close friendship. This gave Mu the support she needed to raise her children with the love and security she herself had never experienced.

The two families went for picnics and meals at each other's homes and eventually there were six children between them. Norman, much older than Sadie, and blind in one eye, was the minister of the tiny Church of St Cyprian in Melbourne Street, North Adelaide. His car had a cranking handle and running boards that we children delighted in jumping on or off as the car slowly moved. Norman genuinely walked the Christian talk: he gave to the poor, sometimes to the detriment of his own family. If someone came to the door begging for food, he was given food or money should there be any in the house. One night, hungrily looking in their fridge for food, I was shocked to find that a piece of mouldy cheese was the only thing to eat. In winter, when there was no money for shoes, their eldest child John walked to Art School in North Terrace in the rain with bare feet.

Norman Crawford, John almost hidden, Robert and Sarah.

Norman was unconventional. He caused shockwaves in the church community in 1943 when he published his small book *Let's be Frank about Sex*. In the foreword, the Bishop of Goulburn writes,

> We are moving away from an age which sought to deal with sex by repression maintained by custom and tabus… The tabu ethic…did enable people to follow a line of conduct even at terrible emotional cost.

Norman wrote about the normality of masturbation and wrestled with the problem of homosexuality with a frankness that was ahead of his time. Jim was not as comfortable with Norman as Mu was with Sadie – not only was he a priest but a psychotherapist and a pacifist. There is perhaps a little hesitation in Sadie's inscription for Mu in Norman's newly published book:

> Our Muriel
> So much love
> to Jim too and 3 bairns.
> From Sadie and the Author.
> Sept 1943

The families were close for several years, with Sadie being a rock of support, nurturing Mu's interest in psychology, child-rearing and education. The date of the inscription, however, with the reference to '3 bairns' is a sad pointer to a tragedy that would unfold when I was two.

My birth on 14 June 1941 at Calvary Hospital was straightforward. Like Robert, I was born with red hair, in contrast to our dark-haired parents. We were tinged by red hair colouring in grandparents on both sides of the family. At ten weeks, I was baptised by the Rev George Shapley at home. According to my parents, I wasn't given a second name as they considered that Christine Ingleton was long enough! Mu apparently had a model baby this time: I fed well and slept through the night at six weeks. Not only that, I was only spanked once in my entire childhood!

Mu said that when she spanked me I looked shocked. I wasn't used to punishment. I was a good girl! I was very well aware of transgressing whenever I overstepped the mark, and developed a strong conscience to prevent that happening.

The first community kindergarten

By now, Australia was well into World War II. Unlike his brothers, Jim could not volunteer to go to war; he was in the 'essential service' of providing cigarettes to Australians involved in the war effort. Len saw the horror of war in New Guinea, where his plane was shot down, while Ray was stationed in Darwin. Mu was fortunate to have her husband at home but it couldn't have been easy for Jim to see his brothers and friends serving while he stayed behind.

Money and resources were tight, and Mu was looking for ways to provide good play and educational experiences for her own and her friends' children. There were no kindergartens that we could go to. Although there were ten free kindergartens in Adelaide and the suburbs, they were only for the poor. The first of the free kindergartens had been set up in Franklin Street in 1904, catering for the poorest city children. Its director was twenty-year-old Lillian de Lissa, who introduced from Italy the Montessori method of teaching young

Robert, Mim and Christine, April 1942.

children. The Kindergarten Union of South Australia had been founded in 1905, independent of government and universities, and soon after, the Kindergarten Training College was opened. But as yet there were no kindergartens for most children. The interest in the poor was to socially engineer their improvement, as is suggested in the following article in which the Kindergarten Union made a rare appeal for help:

> The main benefits of this training have been received by those children in the community who are most handicapped by poverty in the unfolding of their powers. To countless numbers of these the free kindergarten is the one bright and hopeful environment, the one glimpse of beauty and order which enriches their lives. To exchange for a few hours a day, the atmosphere of a drab street for the serene air of delightful studies, is their only chance of childhood's right to natural mental and moral development. The lives of these children have grown harder and more stunted in these days of wide-spread unemployment, and the Kindergarten Union has added care for the hungry and ill-clad to its ordinary tasks.
>
> *The Register News-Pictorial*, Adelaide, 17 October 1930

It was well after the end of the war in 1945 that kindergartens began to be set up for children who were not poor, when a middle-class push for early childhood education exploded across Australia and overseas. But in the early 1940s, if Mu wanted her children to go to kindy, she decided she would have to organise one herself. She had heard there was a newly established community kindergarten in Melbourne:

> The value of community kindergartens had already been proved at Albert Park in Melbourne where one is being conducted very successfully.
> *The Advertiser*, Wednesday 18 February 1942

With this model in mind, Mu and her friend Mrs Stretton visited the director of the Adelaide Gowrie Kindergarten at Thebarton, a demonstration and model child centre which had opened in 1940 with federal government funding. Although there was no financial support available for a community kindergarten, there was advice from both the Gowrie and the Kindergarten Training College. Over several visits, Mu observed how the kindergarten operated, took details of the daily routines and patterns of play and learning, and advice on how to implement the requirements for an independent community kindergarten with a trained teacher. A bold experiment was under way. A reporter tabled this interview:

> Mothers to Conduct Kindergarten at Edwardstown
>
> An interesting experiment in community kindergartens is to be conducted at Edwardstown by a group of women living in the district. Organiser of the scheme and first president of the mothers committee is Mrs J.M. Ingleton who has two young children. Mrs Ingleton said that because there were few educational opportunities in the district for preschool children she decided to interest other mothers in the idea of providing their own kindergarten. Already there were about 30 prospective pupils and it is hoped to open the kindergarten, which will be undenominational, next month. It will be held in the Church of England Hall, South Road, and will be open from 9 a.m. to midday daily for children from two to six. Mothers who could pay a small fee for their children would do so, Mrs Ingleton said, and these fees would pay the rental of the hall and the teacher's salary.
>
> The committee, Mrs Ingleton said, were very grateful to Miss Hazel Harrison, principal of the Kindergarten Training College, who had given expert advice in planning and equipping the kindergarten.
> *The Advertiser*, Wednesday 18 February 1942

Two months later, not only were enrolments taken, but mothers were also invited to a talk by Sadie Crawford at our home, so beginning an education program for parents.

Proposed Edwardstown Kindergarten

Mothers at Edwardstown who are endeavoring to establish a community kindergarten have arranged for centres to be opened for the enrolment of pupils so that the committee may have an idea of the number of children likely to attend. Mrs. J. M. Ingleton, president of the mothers' committee, said yesterday that next Monday members of the committee would be at the Baby Health Centre Edwardstown between 2 and 4 pm to enrol pupils, and on the following Tuesday, Wednesday, and Thursday at the Church of England hall South road, Edwardstown... Mothers of the pupils will provide funds for equipment, and each has volunteered to work one day a week at the kindergarten under the direction of a trained teacher. At Mrs. Ingleton's residence 9 Railway Terrace Edwardstown at 2.30 p.m. on Friday Mrs. Norman Crawford will give an address on 'Understanding Our Children' which will be followed by discussion.

The Advertiser, Wednesday 22 April 1942

Five weeks later, the first community kindergarten in South Australia was opened.

Mothers Organise Own Kindergarten

Stressing the value of kindergarten work in a war-torn world, the chairman of the executive committee of the Kindergarten Union of SA (Lady Bonython) congratulated the mothers of the Edwardstown district on their good work, when she opened the Community Kindergarten in the Church of England Hall, South Road, on Saturday. The centre, which will be known as the Community Pre-School, bas been organised, and is run by the mothers of the district, who have supplied all the equipment, much of which they made themselves. The president of the committee (Mrs. J.M. Ingleton) welcomed Lady Bonython, and the principal of the training college (Miss H. Harrison) proposed a vote of thanks. Mrs. C.W. Osborne is in charge of the kindergarten, and after the opening ceremony visitors saw the children at work. The sum of £9 was raised by afternoon tea and a jumble stall.

The Advertiser, Monday 1 June 1942

The kindergarten moved into the Clarence Park Institute in March 1946. At its opening on a sunny Saturday morning, I, nearly five, stood in my best dress, in awe at seeing my mother giving a speech.

Despite spearheading the community kindergarten movement in South Australia, Mu felt acutely her own lack of education, having completed only the Qualifying Certificate at the end of Grade Seven. In the city there were only four high schools: Adelaide, Unley, Woodville and Norwood. As for tertiary education, families sent their sons to university but rarely their daughters. Even a generation later, Ron Close was to say to Jim that a university education would be wasted on me, as I would 'only get married'. Ron was the deputy principal of Adelaide Teachers College at the time, the 1960s. However, my Walford headmistress, Miss M. Jewell Baker, had taught me otherwise. At morning assembly, she always gave a short morality talk, often about good manners. She had founded the school to educate young women, and instilled in us the maxim 'An educated boy is an educated man. An educated girl is an educated family.' Mu wanted a good education for her children. She loved reading and intelligent conversation. Her bookshelves held titles on health, childcare, gardening, Australiana and popular novels; there was little on sewing, knitting or crafts! Neither she nor I were particularly keen on the latter, but we did become an educated family.

The family was expanding. Not long after the successful opening of the first community kindergarten, Mu was pregnant again. While working at the kindy, she was preparing for the arrival of her third child, due in September 1943. The new life of that spring, however, was short-lived.

On a grey wintry day in 1943, Robert and I were sitting in the back seat of the car, Jim driving, Mu silent in front.

For the last week, Robert had been asking, 'Where's da baby? Where's da baby?'

Now the red-bricked Children's Hospital loomed in the rain. The new baby, Julie Ruth, had been admitted at the age of six weeks.

Jim with our first car.

Starting with a cold, she developed an ear infection. Then, with a high temperature, pneumonia set in. Due to the war, there was no penicillin available and antibiotics had not yet been invented; there was no medication to fight her illness. A few days later, on 22 October, Julie died. The death certificate reads, 'Death due to broncho-pneumonia and left otitis media'. That drive to the hospital is my earliest memory.

As our small family walked along the shiny white hospital corridor, a sister said to Mu and Jim, 'You're lucky! At least you have two other children.' Lucky!

At the funeral, Jim carried to the graveside the tiny white coffin, not much larger than a shoebox. The death of this baby, when I was only two, has always been present in my life. For Mu, it must have rekindled the tragic loss of her own mother and baby.

Not long after Julie's death, Mu's GP advised, 'Have another baby – as soon as you can. It will help you get over this loss.'

It was the last thing Mu wanted to hear. But, fifteen months later, she was pregnant again. I was three and a half and Robert five and a half when Patricia Judith arrived on 3 January 1945. Alarmingly, she was born a 'blue' baby, indicating oxygen deprivation. The blueness at birth may have intimated health problems to follow, but not yet. Judy was a very pretty baby, with red curly hair, delicate fingers, and

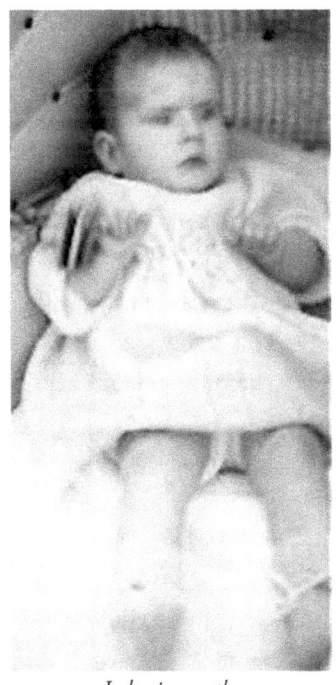

Judy, six months.

eyes that turned an unusual tawny colour. She was much admired by passers-by as she lay propped up in her white wicker pram.

By the time she was six months old, however, she still had to be propped up, showing no inclination to sit on her own. Mu noticed several differences in her development compared with her older children but the GP dismissed her concerns as those of an anxious mother, simply advising her to wait and to stop being over-anxious.

By the age of six, Robert had developed a stammer. Mu wondered what could have caused this. Was it the terrible fright Rob got when a big dog jumped up at him in the pusher one day? The doctor thought this could have been the cause but Norman the psychologist was sure this could not be so. Whatever the cause, Robert's sensitivity was not helped by the new leather school bag he got for Christmas after he turned six, designed to be worn on his back. It was handsome, but it was different: the leather bag was green. 'Greenbags, greenbags!' was the taunt as he caught the nearby bus up Cross Road to Highgate Primary School.

Another problem was my eyes. They were crooked. The left eye looked to the left no matter where the other one looked – I had a squint. At four, I started wearing glasses with the right lens covered to force the muscles of the left eye to work harder. Photos from this time worry me now to see the serious child with straight red hair, freckles and glasses! Less than two years later, however, the dreaded glasses were lost in an accident. I was talking to the girl next door over the high corrugated-iron fence. She had a new doll, a beautiful doll with a soft body, a celluloid head, and eyes that closed. Eagerly I climbed up onto the seat of my tricycle so I could peer over the fence. I had just glimpsed the doll when the trike started moving. I fell straight onto the corrugated iron, slicing my chin open. I ran inside screaming, blood pouring down my dress. In the kitchen, Jim was steadying a ladder for his friend John Rayment, who was up high repairing the ceiling. Mu rushed in, swabbed the wound, replaced the large flap of hanging skin and firmly plastered it down. The doctor advised it would be best to leave the plaster in place and let the healing begin without the benefit of stitches. The scar can still be seen.

Back home again, we realised that I was no longer wearing my glasses. Everyone searched the garden along the fence but happily for me they had really disappeared. Nearly two years later, when a final clean-up of the garden was taking place, Jim's spade hit a foreign object, and the old metal-framed glasses, cracked and crooked, were unearthed. Perhaps the squint had improved, for I no longer had to wear those hated spectacles.

At twelve months, Judy was sitting up but not crawling, and was not alert. There was definitely something amiss. The GP detected a

Judy, aged one.

heart murmur, and further tests showed there were two holes in the heart that would normally have closed over at a few months of age. Judy's slow development was put down at that time to her heart abnormality. At two, she was neither walking nor talking. She grizzled and cried in her playpen and had to be picked up constantly to pacify her. There was little relief for Mu and nowhere to turn for help.

Jim, Mu, Robert and Christine, 1944.

6

Grange

In 1947, Jim decided that he could afford to move his family to a better area and so the house and garden were prepared for sale. Judy was nearly two when we moved to 12 High Street, Grange. The house still stands squeezed between its neighbours, a small villa with a central passage, three bedrooms on one side, lounge, dining room and kitchen on the other, and an enclosed sleep-out, bathroom and laundry at the back. The toilet was outside, but joined to the house.

Like its neighbours, number 12 had a backyard with a Hills hoist, lawn, garden, woodpile (with witchetty grubs!), vegie patch, flower garden and a chook yard. The garage was out the back where big gates opened onto a bumpy grassy lane that passed behind everyone's yards. In earlier years, the network of lanes all through the suburb had given the night carts access to each property's toilet, the outside dunny,

12 High Street, Grange, 2014.

before the sewage system had been established. Now the lanes offered pedestrian short cuts between all the streets as well as giving access to garages at the backs of the houses.

These were the immediate post-war years. Although the war had ended in 1945, supplies and money were scarce. Mu made many of our clothes, including our underpants. She darned all our socks, mostly in bed on Sunday nights listening to the radio, turned shirt collars, re-used buttons from clothes no longer wearable, and carefully made savings wherever possible. Her old Minties tin filled with buttons remains a grandchild's treasure. Coupons were issued for all essential items, limiting families to specific quantities of goods such as butter, meat, clothing and petrol. Gas strikes, meat strikes and train strikes had to be endured.

At seven, I was old enough to go to the shops. One day, Mu sent me to the butcher's on Grange Road to buy some lamb for dinner. I couldn't remember what sort of chops she wanted, so chose her favourite, loin lamb chops. I can still remember the butcher's surprise but he cut the number I asked for. When I got home, Mu was angry. I had spent the whole week's meat coupons on the luxury of loin lamb chops for one meal! Likewise, Robert hasn't forgotten the furore he caused when he lost the butter coupons one day. No wonder our generation is so careful with money and food!

A diary fragment

The house at Grange was not Mu's choice but Jim said it would be 'Only for five years, dear.' However, the ten long years that ensued were not happy for Mu – she said she hated living there. Now a big surprise comes into my story, suggesting a clue to her unhappiness. In a New Year clean-up, in 2014, my son Steve unearthed a torn, lined exercise book from a carton of old papers in his shed. This forty-six-page book has no covers and is barely held together by its linen threads. The first six pages have pasted newspaper cuttings dated by hand 1938. They include items about the royal family, Miss Beryl Pointon to marry Mr Gordon Brown (a friend), Howard Hughes's plane landing in New

York, and the half-ton birthday cake for the Hindmarsh centenary celebrations (a reminder of Harry?).

Much of the book is empty until unexpectedly a diary appears, dated from 1/1/47 to 28/6/47. For six months, there is a daily entry written in fountain pen in Mu's flowing, confident hand. A few pages towards the end are written in pencil. The last page is torn, and it looks as if other pages have been torn out. The diary ends as suddenly as it begins. Sometimes it appears that several days have been filled in at once (is that why my birthday wasn't mentioned?) but few dates are left blank. Was the keeping of the diary a New Year's resolution? Did someone suggest that Mu keep a diary for six months to keep a steady hold on her life? Was it therapy? She often used to advise, 'Write down what or who you're unhappy about, then burn it!'

This is how the entries in the first two pages of the diary appear:

Midnight 1st January 1947. (Wednesday)
Chris, Jim & I. (Judy asleep, Robert at Strathalbyn).

2nd Judy not well. (Measles maybe,)

3rd Jan. Fri Judy's birthday (2 years). Christened by Rev Shapley. Mrs Shapley and the Reg Vennings present. (Judy a little better.)

4th Sat a happy day for all. Mrs Venning and I went to Town. (bought sandals). Beach all afternoon, cards at night – bed 11 p.m.

5th Sun Very hot day. The Maynes came. The Vennings went home after a stay of five days.

6th Jim went back to work. Wrote to Maisie. (Pop 30 pounds). Judy quite better. Met Mary Welsh.

7th Nothing exciting happened. Pat and Vic [next door neighbours] for dinner. Jim went to bowls at night.

8th Raining in morning. Went on the beach after lunch, lovely then.

9th A letter from Rob at Strath. Helen and Peter for the day. Presents from the Vennings. A chicken out. Spent the evening with Pat.

10th Took Judy to Town to collect her surgical boots. Very hot day. The chicken died.

11th Robert arrived back from Strath 11 a.m. Went to Mrs Fairweather's home this afternoon to see the frangipani and took Mrs Smith with me.

Had a very enjoyable time. Helen there too. Saw the Walking Postman on Main North Road who is walking from Fremantle to Sydney. Jim minded the children. Letter from Maisie.

12th Jan. Sunday. Pop [Jim's father, Grandpa James] and Ruby called for half an hour. (30 pounds). Robert and Chris on beach as usual. Jim and I took Judy for walk. Vic came and listened to play. Wrote to Tiny. Mrs Edwards made pearl bracelet for Chris.

13th Washed this A.M & ironed. Prepared apricots for preserving. Letter from Grandma, [Jim's grandmother Jane, aged 88] coming Wed. Pat came in for a chat this afternoon.

14th Helen & Patricia came, left Peter and took Chris. Had hair set and Chris' cut. Vera P went to the Jackson's for week or two. Jim at bowls tonight. Pat stayed with me.

15th Talked to Vera P over phone. Grandma and Aunt Rose for lunch. Rang Christine. Norman C rang. Advised that Robert be sent to Olive Abotomey for speech training. (stammering badly) Beth rang.

16th Vera P came for a morning cuppa. Rang Olive A.

(Gas strike in 6th week)

I noticed first the number of people in and out of the house every day, some staying for a few days. Mu was rarely without the company of other adults, especially in the evenings Jim was out. Old friends and neighbours kept visiting or ringing, many of them remaining in touch for the following decades. But how was Mu managing? There is only an occasional acknowledgment of her feelings:

28th Jan A very hot & dusty day. Life in general very dull. Feeling 'down'. More than I can cope with. Must see the Dr. Jim at bowls again. (Letter from Tiny [Pearce].)

10th Feb Took Judy to Dr Bowler to have tummy strapped – had overhaul myself. Must have chest XRd. Went to Majestic with Jim, saw 'Stolen Life' (Bette D).

March 7th No 10 for lunch. Joan [next-door neighbour] spent afternoon with me. Joan getting married this year, will miss her very much. Have been invited to a bridge evening at Mrs Jackson's on Tues. night – may brighten my dull life socially.

I cannot escape a flatness of tone that suggests depression. Although so many people were calling in and phoning, and Mu was going out to play bridge and table tennis, and occasionally to a movie or show, her life felt dull.

> 18th Mar Had afternoon tea at Mrs Jackson's. Ivy came for dinner. Going to show with Mrs Jackson tomorrow night. Phone calls from Joan, Vera, Helen & Ivy & Mrs Graves. Rang Doss [Shapley].
>
> 19th Had afternoon tea with Mrs Jackson and Anne Lane. Went to see 'Johnny Frenchman' (film) at York with Mrs J. Pop came to see Jim. Letter from Grandma.
>
> 20th Thurs Vera rang today. Spent day with me. Jim dining at the L.V. Elliott's. Barbara Roads came to stay for few days while mother in hospital.

Despite the war, Ingleton hospitality was generous, and hard times made people pull together to help each other. On 8 February,

> Colin Smith came in after we were asleep with the sad news of Lorna's death (suddenly at Roxy Theatre) heart. Stayed with Mrs Smith till 3 a.m.

There is mention of Lorna coming in to ring just four days earlier. On the day after the funeral, her husband Max came to discuss the use of the sleepout, and with the help of Max, Grandpa and neighbour Vic, the sleepout was furnished and wired. A week after Lorna's death, Mu helped Max pack up his wife's clothes, and three days later, on 18 February, Max moved in.

Two months later, Max moved out to live with his mother. Grandpa James (Pop) immediately moved in, heralding an unhappy time for all. He was a grumpy old man! His coming was not entirely unexpected:

> 20th Jan Pop continued with cupboards. (Domestic life there (Pop's) threatening to smash).
>
> 19th Mar Pop rang this morning. His wife left him!

On the day he moved in, the diary simply says,

> 24th Apr Pop came to live with us.

One day I peeped through the sleepout window to see if Grandpa James was asleep. 'What are you looking at, little girl?' he gruffed at me and I slunk away. What a shame he was the only grandparent I ever knew! Grandpa drank too much, and was an embarrassment when he fell off his bike in High Street on the way home from the pub, smashing several bottles of beer on the road. He spent three months at a time with Jim, Ray and Beth over the next years until he was diagnosed with dementia and moved into the Northfield wards of the Royal Adelaide Hospital, where he died in 1962.

While Grandpa was living with us, Mu was always busy cooking, baking, preserving, knitting jumpers for each of the children and gardening.

26 Jan My vegetable garden very successful, picking beans, tomatoes, cucumbers, sweetcorn & spinach.

And on 24 March,

Still reading 'The Robe'.

I can't imagine she had much time to read, even though she loved books.

In February 1946, Robert and I began attending Grange Primary School, with its traditional red brick classrooms, tall windows and asphalt playground. Lunches packed, homework in our school bags, Robert and I left to walk to school along High Street, joining up with other kids along the way. Mu's days were filled with looking after Judy and managing the constant chores of washing, cooking and cleaning. Coming home from school, I dreaded finding scribble on the walls or discovering what might have happened in my absence. One morning as I packed my school bag, I saw scribble on the front of my Grade One memo book and cried. Nothing was safe. There was no privacy in our shared bedroom. Even when I knelt down to say my prayers one night, Judy interrupted to ask what I was doing. That certainly took all the patience out of my meditative attempt!

Chris, Mu and Grandpa, 1955.

The classes were large and Robert's Grade Four/Five class had a sadistic teacher who picked on him. This teacher forced him to read aloud, then ridiculed him when he stammered. Jim was furious, took Robert out of school and threatened to sue the Education Department, but his friend Ron Close counselled against it, saying he would never win a case against the department. Despite the cost and sacrifice to the family budget, Mu and Jim turned to private schooling and sent Robert to Pulteney Grammar in Grade Five. He proudly went to school with Dad in the company car each morning.

After a short time, my jealousy spoke up: 'I want to go to a private school too!'

Taking advice from the headmaster of Pulteney, Rev. W.R. Ray, Mu and Jim enrolled me at Walford House, far away at Unley Park, where I was accepted – once my parents and I had been interviewed in the headmistress's drawing room. Miss M. Jewell Baker did not accept just anyone in her school, particularly when no other relatives of the child had attended there, so we were dependent on Rev. W.R. Ray's referral. Recently I visited this very room on the ground floor of the two-storey residence still used at Walford, and found little had changed. In the second term of Grade Three, not quite eight years old, I started at Walford, leaving home before eight a.m. to drive into the city with Jim and Robert, so proud in my navy and gold uniform. Then I waited at the tram stop in the middle of King William Road at the North Terrace intersection to catch a tram to Unley. The tram went down Wakefield Street past St Aloysius College, Adelaide's premier Catholic girls' school.

Such was the prejudice in those days that we Walford girls looked down on the Catholic girls in their purple uniforms (purple was such a Catholic colour!) and even further down our noses at the state school girls going to Unley High, untidy in their much less disciplined uniforms. We of course wore blazers, hats, gloves and thick lisle stockings, and woe betide any girl whose uniform was incomplete, whose dress was shorter, or hair longer, than regulation, or who wore a pullover without a blazer. Being caught defying any of these rules meant punishment by an order mark tallied against one's House. My House was Gordon, and I was given my only order mark when the head prefect, Gillian Cashmore, spotted me eating in the street one afternoon. I had bought my favourite candy bar, a White Knight, from the popular deli by the tram stop in Grenfell Street, to tide me over the tram journey to the Henley Beach terminus, followed by another half hour walking home to High Street. I was in Year Eight then and it took me one and a half hours to get home from school each day.

Disability

Robert and I were settled into our new schools, but Judy wasn't at all settled. At Grange, Mu had an excellent GP, Dr Odlum, who tested Judy thoroughly and referred her to a physiotherapist. The physio was one of Adelaide's leaders in the field of understanding left–right brain development through movement. A new approach to psycho-motor patterning was being developed, called the Delacato method, which she may have been using. The physio visited regularly and drew up a comprehensive program for Judy. I often came home from school to find a large woman crawling along the passage moving Judy's arms and legs alternately to imitate a crawl. The passage went straight from the front door to the back (one of the reasons Mu disliked the house), so Judy's exercises with the physio meant we had to step around the pair on the way to the kitchen and bedroom and then keep well out of the way. After school, we usually had a snack and listened to the small green bakelite radio on the kitchen bench. (One delicious snack was bread spread with dripping saved from the Sunday roast.) Nobody enjoyed those twice-weekly visits and for Judy they were torture. As she couldn't talk, she screamed, struggled and cried out in her frustration.

Slowly, however, the physiotherapy worked. After a few months, Judy started crawling independently. At two years and two months, she took her first step. She learned to walk, but her ankles were weak and her feet were twisted. Within weeks of starting to walk, she had surgical boots made to give her ankles strength and to straighten her feet. They had to be worn every day for several hours, but they hurt terribly. Whenever we went out, Judy had to be dressed against her will, kicking and screaming against the dreaded boots. The pain, the yelling and the resistance exacted a toll on all of us.

When Judy was three, she was walking and beginning to talk. Her new-found mobility presented her with an unexpected means of escape. A concrete ramp led up a slight incline to the single front gate, which was kept latched. One afternoon, little Judy disappeared. Racing out the front, we saw a crazy pile of things up against the front gate. At the bottom of the pile was a stool; on top of the stool was a kitchen chair; and on top of the chair balanced a trike. Over the trike was freedom! But there was no small child in view. Mu sent us out on our bikes while she rushed into the neighbours before searching the streets. I was in tears riding along High Street when the headmaster rode past on his bike.

'What's the matter, little girl?' he asked, slowing down.

'My sister's run away and we can't find her,' I sobbed.

He nodded. 'I hope you find her soon,' and rode on.

After cycling miserably around the surrounding streets, I arrived home to find that Mu had called the police. They door-knocked the surrounding streets, and in Beach Street at about five p.m. they discovered Judy happily enjoying cordial and cake in an old lady's house. She had seen Judy wandering, and called her in to keep her safe. By the time Jim got home at five past six, calm had been restored and we three children were sitting at our small table eating the evening meal.

The next time Judy disappeared, we couldn't find her at any of the neighbours or along the streets, and I was frightened. Coming home distraught, I went into the bathroom. Shock! There she was hiding behind the bathroom door where she'd been standing mutely pleased with herself for over an hour. I was furious! Judy has a much better developed sense of humour than I, and can laugh heartily at others' misfortune. The joke was on us, but I was already far too serious to appreciate it!

Sometimes, Judy delighted in running out into the street with no clothes on; we never knew what would happen next. When on rare occasions Mu and Jim went out in the evening to a friend's place for dinner or a party, they waited until Judy was asleep then crept out the front door quietly, giving us a phone number to ring if necessary. Robert and I were then aged about ten and twelve. We desperately hoped that Judy wouldn't wake up. When she did, she called out for Mu. If there were no answer, she got out of bed and went down the passage searching. When she discovered our parents were gone, she screamed until they came home in response to our frantic phone call. There was nothing we could do to calm her down.

Mu bore the brunt of Judy's frustration. As it was hard for her to go out to do the shopping, I did most of the errands from the age of seven, taking a note to the corner store, butcher shop and deli. With his stammer, Robert avoided shopping if he could. Bread and milk were delivered daily, and groceries once a fortnight by Mr Vale, who amazed us by deftly unpacking everything with one hand and a stump. Each week, the greengrocer's truck made its way down the street, and I felt privileged climbing up the high steps into the back of the truck to select the fruit and vegetables with the help of Mr Curtis the greengrocer. Judy loved his visits too and called him Cirku. Occasionally the rabbit-o's horse and cart came down the street, the old rabbit-o calling out, 'Rabbits! 2/6 a pair!' and we were excited to buy two freshly skinned rabbits for Mu to make into a mock-chicken stew.

In the small cottage opposite our house lived a piano teacher, Mrs Harvey, with her son Vaughan. We admired Vaughan because at the age of sixteen he was practising deepening his voice in preparation for a career in radio. He succeeded, became a well-known announcer and established the Vaughan Harvey Radio School. Mrs Harvey offered to teach me and I am indebted to Mu for agreeing even though we had no piano. I was invited to practise at Mrs Harvey's. It was daunting knowing she could hear every note I stumbled over at the piano in her lounge room, even though she retired to the kitchen whenever I came over. This is where my music education began. I didn't hear classical music at all on the radio at home, but Mu and Jim enjoyed playing records on their magnificent radiogram, now at Sally's house. They specially enjoyed their record of the folksong, 'When I was a bachelor, I lived all alone.' It was banned in the 1950s for its immorality: the bachelor ended up living alone with his son!

When Judy turned four, Mu looked to the Lady Gowrie Kindergarten for help, and was able to enrol her there for two or three sessions a week. The exhausting and embarrassing journeys by tram were a trial, as Judy struggled against her boots and having to sit still. At home, Mu was battling. The laundry troughs were never empty. Although we had upgraded from a copper to a washing machine, the washing still had to be heaped out of the machine with a long wooden stick, dragged into the trough to be rinsed with Reckitts Blue, then fed through the wringer that could swallow an arm in a moment of inattention. The grinding noise of the agitating machine on a Saturday morning is still with me.

Saturday mornings were hard. I helped Mu with the washing while she did the vacuuming. Judy wasn't toilet trained and so the washing and cleaning seemed endless. I complained of growing pains in my legs that were particularly bad on those mornings and I still loathe the sound of a vacuum cleaner. Jim came home from work in time for lunch, then went straight to bowls in the afternoons. Eventually he gave bowls up to try to support Mu, but this wasn't easy for a person who loved sport.

Before we were old enough to play Saturday afternoon sport, Robert and I escaped to the corner house, where the local real estate agent lived in comparative wealth. Their only child Denis had the biggest collection of comics we had ever seen, piled up in heaps on top of an old woodstove, screened behind a lace curtain. What a treasure and delight! We played lots of games there, but mostly I remember being the witch whom the boys surrounded to burn at the stake, or It in games of chasey. One day, Mu was horrified to find us out the front, the boys rolling a car tyre along the street with me curled up inside it. I didn't appreciate what the fuss was about – it was scary fun!

With Robert's friends one Saturday afternoon, I crawled under the wooden fence of St Lawrence's Home for the Aged at the far end of High Street. Under Denis's instructions, we rolled and smoked foul-tasting cigarettes made from paper and grass while we spied on the old people from the safety of the gum trees. Mostly, though, I tried to be good at home by helping in the kitchen, answering the phone, running errands and keeping the peace.

Minda

The burden of everyday living was becoming too much for Mu's health. Her GP counselled that a place should be found where Judy could be looked after and provided with appropriate activities and schooling. Mu resisted this but she was exhausted. In 1951, she and Jim placed Judy in residential care at Minda Home, Brighton. Judy was six. Night after night, I could hear the muffled sobs from my parents' bedroom as Mu grieved for giving up her child. I cannot imagine the depth of her pain, echoing her own abandonment through her mother's death, and the loss of her own baby eight years earlier.

> Minda is named from an Aboriginal word meaning 'a place of shelter and protection'.
>
> For seventy years [from its inception in 1898], Minda would be the only residential facility in South Australia providing exclusively for people who were intellectually disabled.
>
> http://www.mindainc.com.au/about-us/history

The old photographs on Minda's website don't reveal the sight that confronted us as a family three months later, when we were allowed our first visit. Three months without a family visit was mandated so that the child could settle in. At the end of the long curving driveway shadowed with massive pines and eucalypts was a building with a veranda enclosed in wire mesh. A crush of children crowded behind it, noses to the wire, hands clinging, to glimpse who was coming down the drive, wondering who would have a visitor today. On that first visit, Judy was brought out to see us, her head shaved to defeat the lice. She looked at us but would not speak.

How we dreaded those Sunday visits. There was high tension in the car as we neared those gloomy pine trees. At the end of the drive, we faced the sight of the same crowds of children with the smell of turps or methylated spirits to get rid of bugs and lice. And there was Judy, face tight, silent, speech lost. We took her to the nearby sand dunes so we could all relax and help her unwind, but it made no difference. Still she would not speak. She wanted to wee, but no amount of time spent squatting could produce a drop. The trauma was unspeakable. None of us had words for it. I could feel my parents' pain and my own dread. Judy spent three years in this home,

> established to provide care, education and special training so the children would have happy and useful lives.
>
> http://history.dircsa.org.au

The experience set her back appallingly. After three years, Mu and Jim could bear Judy's distress no longer. They brought her home again when she was almost nine.

Today, Judy's key memory is of her dad coming to visit, and of being toilet trained. She hated the toilet training and all the pine trees. It amazes me that both Rob and I have no memory of her return, or even of how the household changed during her absence and after her return. 'I've wiped all that,' says Rob now.

Judy's return was overshadowed by the onset of Robert's illness. With an extremely high temperature, vomiting and pain in the limbs, he had searing nightmares of flaming asteroids rushing terrifyingly into his eyeballs. It was 1954 and he had contracted polio.

> In the 1950s polio was every parent's greatest dread. It's difficult now to imagine the fear that swept through Australian communities each time there was another epidemic. Thousands of children spent months in special isolation wards, unable to breathe outside the 'iron lungs' that kept them alive.
>
> smh.com.au/news 2004/12/0

Mu made us promise not to tell anyone that Robert had polio, especially when we went visiting. It was a big secret. One day Mu, Jim and I were invited to the beautiful home of the Nesbitts, family friends.

At the top of the stairs I whispered to Mrs Nesbitt, 'We've got a secret!'

'Have you, darling? What is it? Can you tell me?'

'Yes,' I whispered triumphantly, 'Robert's got polio!'

The secret was out. What did Mu say? How did the Nesbitts react? I don't know, but I've never forgotten that I was the one who told the secret. Recent commentary on the polio epidemic of 1954 suggests that

> Polio engendered great fear in our community. There were bigger killers and more common ailments, but the prospect of paralysis and permanent disability were especially terrifying, particularly in a nation which prided itself on its outdoor, sporty lifestyle.
>
> http://www.abc.net.au/time/episodes/ep11

Robert's right leg was affected, but after weeks of rest followed by physiotherapy he gradually recovered its full use without permanent damage. It's hard to imagine how Mu coped with Robert's polio and

Judy's homecoming, and what it was like reintegrating Judy back into the family. Soon, however, Mu was looking for a school that would cater for children with an intellectual disability.

This was the beginning of a step-by-step process over the next thirty years of 'What are we going to do next?' It was hard to find information or resources to support people outside the mainstream. Having a child with a disability wasn't talked about; it was a hidden problem. While Mu spoke freely to other women about Judy, Jim was not comfortable discussing his home situation. Men especially didn't talk about personal things. At a work dinner one night, Mu sat next to one of Jim's colleagues and told him about Judy. To her amazement, that colleague also had a daughter with an intellectual disability but no one at work knew about it. This conversation opened up a bond between the two men, and perhaps enabled Jim to soften towards this daughter.

Judy and I went back to Minda recently at her request to see the transformation from those days to the present attractive small group houses overlooking the ocean, and to feel the genuine care given by the house mothers to each resident. I was amazed that after this visit, Judy was keen to join a craft class there, but she was not eligible because she was now living independently. She was 'far too good' for Minda now.

'What next?' was answered by Mu's discovery of an opportunity class at Ethelton Primary School taught by Miss Rhyll Wertheimer. Rhyll was caring, affectionate, humorous, middle-aged and very experienced. The thirty children she managed suffered a wide range of mental and physical disabilities, and to her delight called her Mrs Worm-tamer. She visited Judy at home and reassured Mu and Jim that Judy could progress in her class. Rhyll became a family mentor and good friend for many years. She also mentored me when I elected to do two weeks' practice teaching in her class in my first year at teachers' college.

Judy caught a special school bus from Grange to Ethelton. Her strongest memory now is of lining up for morning assembly. After 'some bloke's speech', the class marched to their classroom, in line, in time to the music from the band. Although she doesn't think she learnt much there, she did have a basic grounding in the three Rs and social skills. When Judy was fourteen she left Ethelton Primary to go to the special class at Port Adelaide Girls' High School by bus. One memorable day, the bus didn't come, and so Judy walked all the way home to Grange, arriving at about five p.m. to a very anxious household. That was an amazing feat.

It was the advent of television at home that provided Judy with the motivation to read, as she pored over the TV pages to find the programs she wanted, *Lassie* being a favourite. Some of the first TV sets in Adelaide were sold by Jim's company, Cornell Ltd, and so our family was fortunate to have the first fridge and TV set in the street. Television was launched in Australia in 1956, and for several months all the screen showed was a wavy black and white ABC test pattern and a lot of snow. Children down the street flocked to the Ingleton house to see the new wonder and watch the test pattern flicker. Judy loved TV, as she does to this day.

What a boon for Mu, to have Judy happily occupied. For me, though, it was disastrous, as the noise was maddening when I was preparing for the public exams in Years 10, 11 and 12, from 1956 to 1958. I had to study in the dining room next to the lounge with the noisy TV. Before the matriculation exams in Year 12 I stayed with the Close family for the peace and quiet to be found in their dining room, where, with their two younger children, Jim and Bill, we did our homework.

With all three of us at school, the routine at home was more settled. Mu insisted that Jim wind down from work each evening by chatting in the lounge over a few sherries. Without this, he would have remained tense, holding the day's work close to his chest. To facilitate the ritual, we children had already eaten early at our own small table in the kitchen. We were then expected to leave our parents in peace so that Jim could relax. The evening sherry ritual, with cigarettes in hand, continued throughout their lives together, although later Jim gave up smoking, and brandy became Mu's preferred tipple.

As we grew older, Saturdays meant school and district sports for Robert and me. Sunday mornings were for church (Robert and I were in the choir and I taught Sunday school from the age of twelve) and the afternoons were for family outings. After lunch on Sundays, a familiar conversation took place in the kitchen, the hub of the household.

'Where would you like to go today, Mu?'

'I don't mind. Where would you like to go, dear?'

'I don't mind. Wherever you like.'

That would bring a sigh and silence from Mu, and some whistling from Jim until Mu made a decision. She made a tremendous effort to get us three children ready to go out, while Jim would get himself dressed and be standing waiting, on time, near the back door, car keys in hand.

We usually visited friends without warning, expecting someone would be at home. After a time, Judy's intuition prompted her to say, 'They're not home, Dad, I can feel it', and often she was right. She came to rely on what she could feel 'deep down' to make meaning; logic was not her strength. There were two families we visited often, Ron and Flo Close at Marryatville, and Tiny and Ben Pearce at Largs Bay. Sometimes we called on Rhyll and her partner Toni, or the families of Jim's brother and sister, Ray and Beth.

Very occasionally, perhaps once a year, we visited Mu's step-grandmother Rose. Rob recalls great-grandfather as an old man with a white beard, while for me the smells, sights and sounds of the cocky's cage and native shrubs remain, and the drip-safe on the back veranda. Grandma Rose sometimes took us over to the cedar chest of drawers to find a florin each. One day, Rose confided to Mu the fact of her own pregnancy at sixteen, giving Mu some insight into her behaviour as a young step-grandmother. Mu was able to forgive her a little then for treating her so badly.

On those Sunday drives, Judy sat between Robert and me in the back seat, squirming and grizzling. On the way home from visiting the Pearces, we often stopped for an ice cream at a deli on Military Road. Mu and Robert or I got out to go into the deli. Then Judy struggled to get out. By the time she stepped onto the footpath, she yelled and pulled away from our hands. How I hated the public humiliation with the shopkeeper and customers looking on. The ordeal over, and settled in the car once again, we drove off in silence, eating our ice creams, stony-faced, looking ahead.

Family holidays were rare. In fact, after marrying, Jim didn't take a holiday for twelve years. Mu pointed this out while dancing with Mr Cliff Cornell one night at a work function, and Jim was soon asked to take the first of his annual holidays. These were mostly spent at home doing maintenance such as house painting and making bookshelves out of packing cases – I still have one of these sturdy bookcases. As he was painting, he taught me one of his working songs that went something like this:

> Slap dash dash goes the whitewash brush
> up against the garden wall.
> In and out the corner, round the jolly 'orner;
> we're a pair of fair old snorers!

Unfortunately, my rendition of this did not go down well with my Grade Four teacher, who in a quiet moment asked if anyone had a song they'd like to sing to the class. 'Thank you, Christine, that's enough. You can sit down now!'

Holidays for Robert and me were church camps, going away with school friends, and spending summer holidays at Berri with Fred and Maisie Bevan on their fruit block. For one family holiday, we drove to Melbourne to stay with Nell (née Taylor) Scott and her family in their then-rural home in Boronia and at their beach house at Sorrento, which is still in their family.

In the years at Grange, Mu employed a cleaner one day a week. Ivy Huckle, a single mother with a young daughter, Chrissie Mary, became a lifelong friend of the family. She became our Auntie I, showering us with buxomy love, managing Judy well, babysitting and providing regular sturdy help for Mum.

Robert and I joined St Agnes's Anglican Church on Military Road

Jim and Mu in Sydney, late 1940s.

at Grange, where we thrived in the clubs that most young people we knew joined in those days: the Girls' Friendly Society for me, the Church of England Boys' Society for Robert, and later the Youth Fellowship. We both joined the choir, which had a few of our GFS and CEBS friends in it, going to choir practice one night a week and sitting in the choir stalls with our friends on Sundays. Denis, our friend with the comics, was the crucifer. He had the privilege, reserved for boys, of holding the cross and leading the choir into the church. I was already a feminist at twelve, complaining to the priest that girls should be allowed to perform the same tasks as boys, such as reading the lessons and assisting at communion. He was thoughtful enough to allow girls to have these privileges too.

Mu went to church occasionally, and always at Christmas and Easter, but I was embarrassed when she left straight after communion, before the service had finished, to put the roast on for Christmas Day. Mu's sweet voice was familiar with most of the hymns but I never heard Jim sing in church. He attended on ceremonial occasions including my confirmation, when he winked at me during the solemn prayers. Being very pious, I was horrified.

On Sunday evenings, specially in winter, there were only three or four of us in the choir, and nine or ten in the congregation. One of the evening regulars was Wilf, who was 'different'. He livened up the sermons by calling out loudly whenever he disagreed with the priest, making an amusing time for the congregation!

Kirkcaldy Beach was only four blocks away, and Grange jetty with all its excitement of jetty-jumping for the boys not much further. We rode our bikes to the magnificent sand dunes of Tennyson, where Robert and I played with friends for hours totally unsupervised but within coo-ee of our friends' house for snacks. A scary escapade I never told Mu about was when we went off on our bikes with Denis to the nearby samphire swamps (now a golf course and housing development). The train, which terminated at Grange, crossed the swamps on a long viaduct. We huddled under a culvert in the middle of the swamp waiting for a steam train to pass overhead.

'Of course,' grinned Denis, 'if a train lets off steam while it goes over us, we'll be goners!'

Thankfully, this terror never happened.

Some of our freedoms were expansive, in contrast to the constraints when it was my responsibility to look after Judy, especially at the beach. Mu was happy when we three children went to the beach to play for a few hours, but then I had to stay in the shallow water with Judy, who was too afraid to go in very far, as she still is today. Of course there was no fun in that, so when possible I sneaked out of the house to go for a swim by myself, dreading Judy catching me before I was safely away. The guilt of being so sneaky still besets me today. Despite that, the beach has remained a wonderful source of beauty, freedom and contentment in my life.

Estcourt House

Although she didn't enjoy living at Grange, Mu developed a strong social network and a large circle of friends. One of her friends, Zona Nelson, was a teacher at Estcourt House on the seafront at Tennyson. The beautiful mansion, originally built for the Estcourt family in 1882, became an annexe of the Children's Hospital for children convalescing from long-term diseases such as polio and perthes. (Perthes is a childhood disorder of the hip where the blood supply fails causing necrosis in the joint. In those days, extended bed rest was required.)

Huge dormitories had large windows overlooking the sea. For months, some of these children lay strapped onto hard, ugly wooden frames where their schooling continued. Those more mobile sat at individual desks to do their school work.

One day, Zona asked Mu if she'd like to work as her assistant teacher now that Judy was at school. Lack of qualifications was not a problem as Mu would be fully supervised by Zona, and she would be subject to annual inspections from the Education Department.

Mu loved this work, and the children loved her. Sometimes I went with her during school holidays watching and helping as she moved from bed to bed and frame to frame. For each child, she had a bright smile, lots of encouragement and compassion. Zona, however, was a stickler for correctness, lacking Mu's warmth and responsiveness. When the inspector came to assess the two teachers, observing their interactions with the children, looking at lesson plans and asking questions, Mu was nervous. Her untrained approach was being assessed by the Education Department! She need not have worried. On 1 August 1956 the Superintendent of Primary Schools, W.V. Leach, sent Mrs M.H. Ingleton Form I/9:

> On reviewing the Inspector's report upon the recent inspection of your work, and other evidence of your efficiency as officially recorded, I have awarded you a skill Mark of 17.0.

The following year, Mu was awarded a skill mark of 21.0, and in 1958 it was 22. This was cause for great satisfaction as her skill marks now exceeded Zona's! Perhaps it was as well for both of them that the Ingletons were soon to leave Grange, upgrading to a pretty art deco house at 21 Sussex Terrace, Hawthorn.

7

Hawthorn

The move to Hawthorn was made possible by Jim's promotion to the board of directors of Cornell Ltd on 12 April 1957. The letters of congratulation that Jim received on his promotion, and the prompt replies typed by his secretary, give some insight into his character – his ability, ready acknowledgement of others' friendship and help in achieving his directorship – and the care with which he drafted his expressive letters.

13 Danido Rd
Springbank SA

12th April 1957

Dear Jim,
    The privilege of friendship prompts me to convey my best wishes to you on your appointment as a director of your Company and to express the wish that you will enjoy many happy years in this new sphere.
    I often look back to those happy days in the YM in association with your good self and your fine brothers to whom I would also convey kind remembrance.
    Yours sincerely
    Tru Barber

17th April 1957

T. Barber Esq.,
13 Danido Road,
Springbank SA
    Dear Tru.,
    Thank you for your delightful letter. I feel very honoured to have heard from you and to have had my thoughts cast back to those happy old YM days.

David Connell, Rory McEwin and Jim Ingleton.

I do not forget Tru that any success I may have had is merely the reflection of the guidance, help and good fellowship that has been bestowed on me by good people like yourself, and I feel truly grateful for the honour of knowing so many good friends.

Please accept my very best wishes and I do hope you are keeping well.

Sincerely yours,

Jim

16th April 1957

K. Doherty Esq.,
c/- W.D & H. O. Wills (Aust.) Ltd
11 East Tce.,
Mile End SA

Dear Kev.,

Many thanks for your telegram and the kindly thoughts expressed therein.

I do want to say Kev how much I have appreciated the help and advice you have given me in the past and that any success I have achieved has only been made possible by the splendid co-operation of good people like yourself.

Yours very sincerely,

Jim

Unfortunately the reply below has been detached from the sender's letter so we are deprived of Mr Don Williams's humour!

17th April 1957

D. Williams Esq.,
c/- John Martin & Co. Ltd.,
Rundle St
Adelaide SA

Dear Don,
　　All rude remarks etc duly noted and appreciated.
　　Would be happy to act in an advisory capacity any time you need to be photographed.
　　Sincerely yours,
　　Jim

The family moved to Hawthorn late in 1959. Mu was thrilled with this house, bought from the owner-builder, Mr Guy. Its rounded wooden front door, so suited to wedding photos, its flowerpot chimneys, lead-light windows, side entrance to the office, and crenellated decoration over the attached garage were just a few of its art deco delights. One of the advantages of being on a corner meant that the baker and milkman could come in the side gate and put their

Mim's Hillman Minx at 21 Sussex Terrace, Hawthorn, 1960.

daily deliveries directly into the customised hatch by the back door. A shoe-cleaning box stood just inside the garage entrance so that we could all polish our shoes for school or work before we got into the car.

In 1959, I was in my first year at Adelaide Teachers College and Robert was working at Clem Taylor's Advertising Agency, having left Pulteney at the end of Year 11. I was wrapped up in my life at Adelaide Uni and Adelaide Teachers College doing a four-year BA and Dip Ed in Secondary Education. I studied hard, ran a babysitting service to raise funds for the Student Christian Movement (SCM) and worked part-time in the Barr Smith Library to supplement (probably illegally) the Education Department allowance that paid my university fees from 1959 to 1962. This allowance was paid back by working for three years after graduation in an Education Department school, Unley High.

Judy was now fifteen and old enough to leave school. Once again the question was, 'What next?' Mu and Jim found a place for Judy in a newly established sheltered workshop. In November 1960, a small group of parents seeking some form of occupation for their children once past school leaving age opened a sheltered workshop in Maud Street, Unley. They had formed the Mentally Retarded Children's Association, the MRCS (now called Orana), in 1958 to enable them to borrow money to establish training and occupation centres for their own children.

> Driven by a powerful belief in the worth and potential of people with intellectual disabilities and by a clear recognition of their right to live valued and productive lives within their own local communities, the Society's Management Committee ambitiously began to establish a range of training, vocational and accommodation services in both the metropolitan and country regions of the State. In the late 1950s and beyond, new services were established where before there had been none, and opportunities were created for people with intellectual disabilities where few had previously existed.
>
> http://www.oranaonline.com.au

Beginning in disused sheds, the parents poured hours of labour into building workshops and finding contracts from suppliers to employ their children in jobs that were self-sustaining. The workshop in Maud Street, Unley, was the first where young people with disability could earn a small wage and work regular hours. A few years later, in 1967, the Commonwealth government introduced a sheltered employment allowance paid at the same rate as the disability pension but structured to allow for earnings (http://history.dircsa.org.au/). Until then, the only available pension for the 'retarded' was for the condition of 'idiocy'.

Mu and Jim became heavily involved in the necessary fundraising and working bees to develop the Maud Street facilities. Judy was sixteen when she started there in early 1961. She tried various jobs such as sorting potatoes and packing eggs to find what she liked and could manage. She enjoyed the social life and made friends there.

Eighteen months later, however, Judy became ill. Jim had dropped her off at her friend Janice's place at Mitcham one Sunday. Janice and Judy had become firm friends at Maud Street. Janice suffered from congenital hydrocephalus. That afternoon, Janice's father, a taxi driver, brought Judy home as she felt so ill. The following Friday, 12 October 1962, Judy was diagnosed with rheumatic fever, and later, chorea. Chorea is a complication of rheumatic fever, and was once known as St Vitus' Dance because of the constant uncontrolled movements of the limbs. More is known about chorea now than we understood then:

> Sydenham chorea (SD) is a neurological disorder of childhood resulting from infection via Group A beta-hemolytic streptococcus (GABHS), the bacterium that causes rheumatic fever. SD is characterized by rapid, irregular, and aimless involuntary movements of the arms and legs, trunk, and facial muscles. It affects girls more often than boys and typically occurs between 5 and 15 years of age. The symptoms of SD can vary from a halting gait and slight grimacing to involuntary movements that are frequent and severe enough to be incapacitating.
> http://www.ninds.nih.gov/disorders/sydenham/sydenham.htm

I can't imagine Mu's life at this time. For months Judy, now aged seventeen, lay bedridden. Mu nursed her full-time, managing her feeding, bedpans and her periods amid her uncontrollable physical movements and facial grimaces. We had to feed her, as the chorea threw her hands about so much. A hospital bed was hired, and a bedpan sourced. Judy lost so much weight and muscle tone that Jim called her Bones, a term of affection they both enjoyed till he died.

One day, Judy had a vision that is as strong for her today as it was then: the Virgin Mary appeared at the foot of her bed, laid her hand on the bed, looked at her and said, 'You'll be all right Judy. You won't die.' From that moment, Judy says, she knew she would get better, and she slowly recovered.

Bedford Industries

With Judy's recovery in 1964, the old question returned: 'What next?' Back to the sheltered workshop, or on to something that offered more scope for her abilities? Mu and Jim looked at Bedford Industries, which in 1950 had taken up property on Goodwood Road, Panorama. Bedford's focus was on 'creating a brighter future for people with a disability through providing work, training and other life opportunities' (www.bedfordgroup.com.au). Bedford was at that time the most forward-looking institution of its kind in Australia, with a strong board of businessmen determined to develop a self-sustaining business model that would enable its clients the dignity of work, income and independence.

Judy started work at Bedford in December 1964. She was picked up and taken home in a small Bedford-owned bus driven by the cheerful one-handed Ron (the other hand having been lost to machinery). She tried out several jobs such as weighing sugar, packing nails and bookbinding. The bookbinding she found difficult but she liked packing nails. Now she was employed again and earning a little money above her pension just as she had at Maud Street. After several months, her supervisor recommended she try an outside job working on the production line at Haigh's Chocolates on Greenhill Road. The Haigh family, living close to Bedford, provided work opportunities for its clients. We all enjoyed a look behind the scenes in the week she was working there, and the chance to buy cheaply the imperfect specimens. Every chocolate was dipped and decorated by hand, so there were a few slips here and there. But Judy found the production line too fast, so her trial was discontinued. Except for Judy, we've all continued to love Haigh's chocolates!

Now Mu put her energy into several areas of voluntary work at Bedford: the cafeteria, teaching literacy skills and fundraising. When Bedford launched its first major fundraiser, the Seal Appeal, she addressed thousands of envelopes by hand to be mailed out. When Jim retired, they did this together. Years later, Mu won first prize in the Bedford lottery, a Holden Gemini. As well, they both supported the work of the Arts Society for the Handicapped. The Arts Society was founded in 1966 at Bedford, and Judy attended painting and drawing classes there. In 1971, courtesy of the City of Unley, the society relocated to the present studio in the historic tram barn on Fullarton Road at Parkside, with its beautiful wisteria-covered arches. Mu worked there one day a week for many years, and we all attended the annual art shows where everyone's work was displayed, and where Judy carried off prizes for her landscapes and abstracts.

Mu's volunteering extended to the local Anglican church, St Columba's, which she and I attended and where I later married Brian Brock. Here she was rostered to drive 'old ladies' to church for midweek services. Two of these ladies were my former headmistress, Miss M. Jewell Baker, and her sister Miss Dob. Apart from communion wine, Miss M. Jewell told Mum, she never drank alcohol. When she went out where alcohol was served, she always drank Pimms No.1! Several charities were supported by Mu's monthly bridge afternoons with old friends from her first years in Adelaide, from Edwardstown, Grange, and now from Hawthorn. Sometimes five tables of four were set up in the lounge and dining rooms, and each month a donation between six and ten dollars was made to a local charity. The game was never serious; it was all about the socialising, the afternoon tea and the bawdy jokes! The bridge parties went on for nearly thirty years and, as everyone grew older, the caring and telephone contact held the women together.

Columbo Plan students

My years at uni brought a new interest into Mu's life: our home became known informally as the 'Vietnamese Embassy' through my friendship with the first group of Vietnamese Columbo Plan students to come to Adelaide. We had scarcely heard of Vietnam then, before the war. In early 1959, the SCM hosted an Asian tea to welcome seven new students to Adelaide Uni and introduce them to local students including freshers like me. There I met the charming, diminutive Vu brothers, Bao and Ky, engineering students who had topped the English entry exam for all of Vietnam; the tall and handsome Nguyen Anh Tuan; and many others. I enjoyed this experience so much that the next Asian tea was held at our house at Grange, shortly before we moved to Hawthorn. Mu and Jim were quite happy to have a crowd of Asian students in their home and to turn over the kitchen to the amateur cooks. Although none of them had done any cooking at home, they appeared proficient and confident, especially as we were totally new to any style of Asian cooking apart from the bland Australian-Chinese fare in Adelaide's few restaurants! There was a lot of rice left over the night of the Asian tea so Tuan wrapped it in a damp tea towel, pressed it firmly and said it would be perfect sliced up cold for a picnic. The next day, a Saturday, two or three carloads of Asian students and I drove to Victor Harbor for that picnic.

While we were still living near the beach, I invited friends to come to Grange for a swim. One day, Tuan's old green Peugeot arrived with Ky, Bao and others for the first of several such visits. Looking out the front window with the blinds half-drawn, Mu could see several pairs of legs by the Peugeot and remarked how pale they all were. They didn't look Asian at all! My parents liked these boys and were quite happy for me to go out with Tuan, often in a group. As new Vietnamese students arrived early in 1960, Tuan brought them home to meet Mr and Mrs I, so called because it was easer to pronounce than Ingleton and less formal.

When Tuan's cousin Dung arrived, his name needed some modification, so a z was added to make Dzung look respectable. On his first visit, he sat in the kitchen at Hawthorn, quiet for a very long time, preparing a pile of green beans to be cooked.

Finally he looked up and slowly asked Mu, 'How...old...are... you, Mrs I?'

We burst out laughing. In Australia, one never asks this; in Vietnam one always needs to know. Mrs I told him, as she wasn't coy about her age. She and I enjoyed exploring the cultural differences that so often caught us by surprise. I also had a close friend, Ling Ai Mee (later Seet Ai Mee), a Chinese Malaysian girl who became part of the family and spent a lot of time with Mr and Mrs I. I still spend time with these friends, as Mu did to the end of her life.

It became a tradition that each year new students were introduced to Mr and Mrs I. One of the new arrivals in 1963 was Tran Van Nguyen, who became a frequent visitor and felt that Mrs I was a mother to him. I asked Nguyen to write a few words about Mu for this story. In this excerpt, he writes,

> Mrs I was petite and beautiful. I would describe her as having an Egyptian mould of beauty. Her face was rounded triangular. Her eyes bore a hint of sadness. But her special smile camouflaged it well. She smiled through her eyes naturally and they were gentle and friendly with us. But I guessed through my careful observation they could become very resolute and determined even when facing a domineering tyrant. She was not the one to become subdued easily. She was a gentle mother. But she could be a fighting mother as well.
>
> Mrs I was one of those Australians who would not have any anxiety about meeting and helping the Vietnamese or other foreign people. I was pleasantly at home with her. The amazing thing was that she seemed to be a person I had met and seen and heard before. She never had to raise her voice to make us understand her. She seemed to be able to adjust her voice automatically according to our subtle facial expression and body language feedback. That was an amazing ability. It was an ability that helped make people feel at ease and enticed people to go on talking as if one was talking to a friend in a normal friendly encounter. She could complete her sentence by a grin, a gentle nod of the head or a hand movement...
>
> Mrs I seemed to be well versed in the Vietnamese customs. She would not accept the first 'no' as a final 'no'. She knew that the first 'no' was the

usual from a culture which did not permit one to say 'yes' straightaway. A prompt 'yes' would indicate greedy and impolite. The teaching in good manners was not to say 'yes' straightaway but to say a 'no' but 'yes' if insisted. It was indeed a very subtle roundabout way of saying 'yes please'. I observed her waiting for a moment then with a gentle grin she offered the food again. We took it by the handful and were thankful for her bit in understanding our cultural courtesy or diplomacy. Very often at other parties the second offer never came and some Vietnamese came home hungry.

Her body was very petite alongside her husband, a big man like Mr I. She was slim and erect even in old age. She was delicate but was full of strength… I often called at her house at short notice when I was in Adelaide. One time I called on her at night while she was already in bed. She did not seem to mind. She actually did welcome the visit. I often interacted with her on the phone. It was wonderful to hear her clear and distinct voice, a voice that helped my overloaded mind to relax. I then let her hear my worries. I felt better after that. She realised too that she had done her bit to help and encourage me to call any time.

Tran Van Nguyen, personal email, 'The Mrs "I" I knew and adored', December 2012

I was in love with Tuan and we went out for about two years before I had to make a decision about where the relationship was going. Could I, a serious Christian, marry a Buddhist? Could I make a life in Vietnam, a country now at war? Could we weather the inevitable intercultural storms? I think he would have risked all that, but I could not negotiate the religious difference. Our splitting up was deeply sad, but we remained friends, and he was still part of the family, loved by Mu and Jim. In mid-1963, he left for home. We had a farewell party at Hawthorn which my new boyfriend Brian came to, and another at Tuan's place the next evening. In Saigon, Tuan married a beautiful Vietnamese woman, had four children, flew to Sydney on the eve of the fall of Saigon, and a few years later appeared on the cover of *Time* magazine with his wife and children as a successful refugee family. He continued to visit the 'I's and me whenever he came to Adelaide, until he died of a heart attack swimming in Sydney Harbour in his sixties.

The Vietnamese friendships tell a lot about Mu's interest in people,

Bao and Annemarie with Mrs I, 1991.

her acceptance and openness, warmth and patience. Jim supported her quietly, and was happy with my relationship with Tuan, but he had some difficulty with the idea of 'our boys' fighting in Vietnam while 'their boys' were having a privileged time here.

When Bao became engaged to Annemarie, a young German student at Adelaide Uni in late 1965, her parents threw her out of home, unable to tolerate her relationship with an Asian. The White Australia policy was still strong in the 1960s. Bao asked if Annemarie could stay with the 'I's until they found a place together, and so Annemarie became another daughter to Mu, a relationship that continued until Mu's death. It was nine years before Annemarie's parents were prepared to get to know their two beautiful grandchildren. In December 1965, Dzung married an Adelaide girl, Mary, and they came to stay for a few days on returning from their honeymoon. Both couples continued their friendship with the 'I's for years.

Grandchildren

By 1962, Mu's first grandchild had arrived. Rob had married Pat Owen and their baby Suzanne Julie (named after Mu's baby Julie) heralded a

Celebrating Mim's fiftieth, 1961. Mim, Jim, Flo and Ron Close.

new generation of Ingletons as well as a new name for Mu. She became Nanna Mim to Rob's children, Suzie, David and Kathryn, and to mine, Sally, Trish and Steve. After Rob and Pat's divorce, Rob remarried. His wife Janet had four children, three of them living in Adelaide, and so Mu became Mim to Janet's children too: Andrew, Susan, Naomi and Simon. Nanna Mim knew six great-grandchildren: Phillip and Elora, Stevie, Maya, Clark, and baby Simone born only eight months before she died. Lucas, Shakira, Ashanjti and Eirinn came later so have missed knowing her.

In 1963, I started teaching at Unley High, close to home, although I had eagerly sought a country post. This placement was chosen for me by Ron Close, who was then deputy principal of Adelaide Teachers College (ATC).

At Unley High, I met Brian Brock, a science teacher, whom I'd known slightly at ATC. He pursued me across the segregated staff room and on his bike, often with a flower in his lapel. We shared many interests and were both keen to spend time teaching in a third world country after our teaching bonds were completed. Late in 1963, before he left to become a teacher in Papua/New Guinea with Australian Volunteers Abroad, Brian and I became engaged. In his twelve months' absence, my social life continued to revolve around SCM and Vietnamese friends. We married in May 1965, with Mim and Jim giving a reception for eighty guests at the once-grand Fernilee Lodge. When I had completed my three years of teaching with the Education Department to fulfil my bond, we left for Zambia. Brian had a three-year government contract to teach science at Chizongwe Secondary School in the Eastern Province, near the Malawi border. In the three years we were away, our Vietnamese friends regularly visited the 'I's.

I don't know how Mim felt about our going to Africa, but she and Jim put no obstacles in our path. Jim was curious about our motivation, which I considered to be altruistic. After all, I had always wanted to be a missionary, and had become a teacher to fulfil that ideal. He shocked me by saying that altruism inevitably had an element of self-interest. I thought self-interest was far from my motivation, but with a businessman's perspective, Jim was more realistic. Now I can agree: there must be a degree of self-interest in all we do! Arriving in Zambia, then a newly-independent country of four million people, I discovered that forty-eight different Christian denominations were at work, and my own Christian missionary pillars shook a little.

We had moved to the capital, Lusaka, when Mim and Jim came for Sally's birth in April 1967. On 28 January that year, Mim flew out of Adelaide alone, on her first overseas trip. Twenty-seven people saw her off at the airport, and ten of Jim's relatives were at Perth airport to say goodbye from there. In Johannesburg, we arranged for a friend to meet Mim, and finally we welcomed her at Lusaka airport. Jim arrived eight weeks later to join us for his two weeks' annual leave. The most difficult part of Mim's journey was not the travel. It was obtaining a passport. She had to apply for a copy of her birth certificate in Broken Hill and she was mortified to have people see that no father was named on it. Mim was in her forties when she confessed to Rob and me that she was illegitimate, and how ashamed she still felt.

As a grandmother in Zambia, Mim was a novelty: there were no white grandmothers among the expatriate community, and she was quickly embraced by our Australian and British friends. To our dismay, however, we had found it difficult to meet black Africans, as so few were teachers and few attended our local Anglican church in Lusaka. We were encircled by the expatriate community. Apart from our house servant Tyson and his family, who had followed us from Chizongwe to Lusaka, there were few Africans for Mim to meet.

At the end of the following year, our Lusaka friends Tony and Judy Gibb stayed with Mim and Jim for a week on their return from Zambia. They visited frequently while we were away, and maintained contact for many years. It's remarkable to me that Mim nurtured such long friendships with so many younger people for the rest of her life.

We returned from Zambia in October 1968 when I was five months pregnant. I stepped off the plane in a maternity dress several inches above the knee, one I'd made on my hand-driven Singer sewing machine. Trish was born at Calvary Hospital in February 1969 just after Brian had started his new job as a lecturer in science at Western Teachers' College. We lived with Mim and Jim for five months, not easy for three generations in a two-bedroom house. We were relieved to finally move into our first home in Mills Street, Clarence Park, on 3 April 1969. That year, Jim took six months' long service leave, taking Mim to Streaky Bay and Berri to enjoy fishing, which she loved. They drove to Perth and Albany, later to Melbourne, Sydney and Bathurst, and in between helped out with child-minding for Rob and me. Mim notes in her small 1969 diary,

> July 18 Chris and babies came at 8.30 a.m. Watched telecast of astronaut in spaceship.
>
> July 21 Neil Armstrong stepped on the moon!

Until Sally was six, we didn't have a TV, on the principle that small children should be active and creative, so the children really enjoyed going to Nanna Mim's and Papa's!

Returning from his Zambian holiday in April 1968, Jim was confronted with a second takeover of his company. Cornell's had first been taken over by APD Tobacco Ltd a few years earlier, and now APD had been taken over by WD and HO Wills. Jim wrote to me in a letter dated 8 October 1967,

> Mum has probably told you that I've had my hands pretty full since our return home with the takeover of APD Tobacco Ltd. Your old man now manages a company with an annual turnover in excess of $12,000,000 per year, the biggest of its kind in Sth Aust. Once again I'm being subjected to a special study course 'The effective executive' and am currently studying and about to be examined on Chapter 2 styled 'Know thy time'. The computer era is here and there is no longer room for the old type experienced bod like myself.

Jim had risen from office boy to managing director. Now that he was part of an international company, he had to attend management courses along with the young, inexperienced graduates proud with their MBAs. His wealth of experience, knowledge and business judgement were no longer relevant to younger executives. He hated those courses, and the pressure of performance was making him sick.

8

Later years

Freedom

Jim retired from Wills on his fifty-ninth birthday in 1970 and immediately started voluntary work with Meals on Wheels. Mim continued to drive older ladies to church, worked at Bedford on Wednesdays, and attended and hosted monthly bridge games. They went to Coffin Bay, Berri and Port Lincoln for holidays and fishing, while Mrs Doyle, who had replaced Auntie Ivy when we came to Hawthorn, stayed with Judy. Judy was proficient with cleaning and gardening chores, and basic cooking – scrambled eggs were her forte. The following year, when I was pregnant with Steve, Brian injured his back during a student camp, culminating in a laminectomy on 17 July 1971 at Ashford Hospital. He was off work for a few months and had only just returned when Steve was born at Blackwood Hospital. With three children under five, I needed support with child-minding, which Mim and Jim gave generously.

Mim was in her sixties when she suffered some broken ribs in a car accident on Cross Road in 1976, and in 1979 a broken wrist from losing her balance while putting on her pantyhose. She had osteoporosis without knowing. However, the broken bones didn't deter her from several fishing expeditions to Coobowie or from going overseas again.

In the 1970s, Mim's international connections continued. She organised a holiday to Singapore in 1972 with Jim's cousin Audrey Maloney, where Mim stayed with Ai Mee and her family and then with Ai Mee's mother in Kuala Lumpur, while Audrey stayed with her son. Audrey was much too keen a shopper, so it was not the easiest of

Ai Mee's family with Jim, Mim and Chris March, 1980.

holidays for Mim. In 1978, Mim took Judy on a Pacific cruise. Judy came home with an infected ear and Mum with pleurisy but there were a few happy memories. Ai Mee's hospitality was reciprocated when she came with her two children and her mother to stay with Mim and Jim in March 1980. In October that same year, Mim and Jim spent over a month in Singapore, Hong Kong, Bangkok, Kuala Lumpur and Malacca. Six months later, they were off again to stay in Singapore and Malacca with Ai Mee and her parents.

Balyana

In 1974, Jim started sessional work with Wills that was to continue for some years, and for Judy a huge opportunity came with the opening of Balyana, a supported residential centre built for Bedford clients. It was a two-storey motel at nearby Clapham, the first of its kind in Australia. For the sum of sixty thousand dollars, a motel unit could be purchased for life, ensuring that residents could be cared for when parents could no longer manage. This seemed to be the ideal 'what next' move, removing all worry from Mim and Jim concerning Judy's future. On 12 May 1974, Judy was one of the first to move in. Mr and Mrs Edwards were the foundation house parents and under Mrs Edwards's supervision, Judy learned the housekeeping skills necessary to work there. Three months later, she was employed as a housemaid and kitchen hand. When the Edwardses' spaniel had a litter of puppies, Mim and Jim brought home a black puppy, Topsy, the last pet in a long line of cats and dogs that had been part of home all my life. Judy came home for weekends and holidays for the first few months, but soon settled well into life at Balyana, living there full time.

Judy's future, however, was not as secure as her family had hoped. In 1980, Mim and Jim were surprised to learn that she was staying in one of the newly built share houses designed to prepare people for independent living, sharing with her friend Michael Shaw. How the move was made without her parents' knowledge is a mystery. But Judy's desire to be married and have a home of her own was a powerful driver. On 29 August 1981, she became engaged to Michael. Despite the family's trepidation about this step, they supported her in having what she badly wanted, a husband and her own home. Throughout her adult life the family has encouraged the development of independence and responsibility, an essential but high-risk approach. Judy never predicted long-term consequences that seemed obvious to others. Of course, the same can at times be said for all of us!

Headstrong, Judy took the initiative and plunged into marriage in search of her dream for a normal life. That was a huge challenge, but what about sex, and having children? These are deep questions for parents of children/adults with disability, especially daughters. Who is responsible for decisions about fertility? Fortunately, Judy was clear about not wanting to have children, so Mim took her to Flinders Medical Centre to discuss and implement a permanent option for contraception.

The next step was to find suitable rental housing through the SA Housing Trust and join the waiting list. A year later, Judy resigned from Bedford. She and Michael were married on 8 January 1983 with seventy guests in the lounge at 21 Sussex Terrace, and a reception in the back garden. Sally and Trish were beautiful teenage bridesmaids in pink. Judy and Michael then moved into their home at Novar Gardens with the help of Michael's half-sister, Glenda, and Mim and Jim.

Another wedding and reception followed theirs only six days later. On Friday 14 January, Rob and Janet (née Gurr) were married in the lounge at seven p.m. Mim's diary says nothing of the preparations the two weddings must have entailed, but on the fifteenth she and Jim went to Sydney for a much-needed holiday, returning on 2 March in time for Mim to give a literacy lesson at home at three p.m.!

Mim was now seventy-two. Her diaries note weekly school visits for the next six months at Katuni, an outpost of Bedford, at Panorama TAFE, and training sessions at the Adult Literacy Unit for home tutoring. (From 1980 to 1985 I worked in the Adult Literacy Unit training volunteers to teach adults reading and writing on a one to one basis – my first regular job, hourly paid, after having the children.) Mim was an ideal home tutor. Over the next four years, her students were David, Simon, Rosemary, Wayne, Wilanie and Yvonne. Some of the lessons were at Panorama, but most students visited her at home, sometimes on a Saturday. In many ways, this was an extension of the work she had done so many years before at Estcourt House. She enjoyed working with young people and knowing the deep satisfaction of helping students learn.

In August 1983, the troubled months of Judy's marriage were over. There had been many problems, not the least of them Michael's gambling and controlling behaviour. Judy had had a hysterectomy in July, staying in hospital for nine days, recuperating at Kalyra for three weeks, then another short spell in Flinders three weeks later. She went home to Novar Gardens on 20 August. But only a few days later she walked out, caught two buses and arrived at Sussex Terrace with a suitcase. She had said no to the abusive relationship. Mim's diary notes,

September 25 1983: Collected Judy's property from Novar Gardens with Glenda.

Not much wonder that Mim soon had a colon attack and was diagnosed with diverticular disease.

In April 1985, Judy's divorce was finalised. The old question of 'what next?' arose again. Bridges had been burnt; the permanence of Bedford and Balyana were lost, and Judy was back at home. After many evenings of discussion while sipping sherries in the dimly lit lounge before their customarily late meal, Mim and Jim called me in. For Judy's independent accommodation and safety, and their own privacy, they had decided to build a granny flat. The existing backyard was divided into two sections separated by a brush fence and tall poplars. The front section was a pretty paved garden with lawn and a Hill's hoist, while the back had a shed and carport. These could be demolished to make room for a flat.

Such a plan required council approval, and that needed a letter to explain the purpose of the granny flat. Would I please write that letter? Would I please explain that their daughter had an intellectual disability and needed secure accommodation? Neither Mim nor Jim had the emotional strength to write the letter asking for permission. I'm not sure of their financial strength either, as most of the sixty thousand dollars had been lost to Balyana, and thousands of dollars worth of Cornell shares given to Dad had proved worthless. In their home office, I drafted a letter to the council for Mim to type. This next step meant long-term commitment. How would it work out?

In March 1984, the foundations for the granny flat were poured and eight weeks later Judy moved in, thrilled with her own one-bedroom fully self-contained unit. Over the next four weeks, twelve visits to the chiropractor ensued, whether for Mim or Jim is not clear in Mim's diary! Now Judy was cooking and cleaning for herself and working for Mim, doing the housework and shopping, and helping to set up the tables and chairs and afternoon teas for the regular bridge parties. Matching the pretty floral cups, saucers and plates wasn't an easy task for her and she felt the pressure of getting everything right for the visitors. Judy was now constantly under Mim's too-critical eye and a fractious co-dependency grew.

Jim was the buffer between them, soothing both when tempers were frayed. He was gentle with Judy where Mim was sharp and hard

Front section of backyard; granny flat built behind right-hand brush fence.

to please. Jim asked Judy to put ointment on his psoriasis when Mim was away, he shared with her the pain of his arthritic hands and feet, and called her Bones with affection. Judy loved that she and her Dad whistled between their teeth in exactly the same way.

Chris, Jim, Mim, Judy, Brian, Annemarie and Bao at Hawthorn, 22 January 1986.

9

Retirement

Losing Jim

'My Jim died suddenly,' wrote Mim on 2 June 1988.

After lunching out with his old YMCA friends that Thursday, Jim came home feeling unwell. Walking through the laundry, he fell to the floor, dead from a heart attack.

'I think Dad's gone!' was all Mim said on the phone.

Steve and I rushed over from our family home in nearby Carlisle Road to find the paramedics trying to revive him. Mercifully, they were unsuccessful or the brain damage on survival would have been dire.

Mim and I followed the ambulance to the Royal Adelaide Hospital – the second time she had made that numb journey.

It was dark by the time we carried the small brown paper bag containing Jim's clothes and watch down the long corridor, out of the hospital, back home to Sussex Terrace. With her stoicism, Mim insisted on staying home alone, and going to bed alone.

Four days later, the large Centennial Park Crematorium chapel was filled with family, friends and associates. Jim's coffin was decorated with his favourite strelitzia, the colourful bird of paradise, which grew in a massive bush outside my old bedroom window at Sussex Terrace.

Mim was seventy-six. Before Jim's death, she and I had been planning a trip to Indonesia at the invitation of the parents of Ica, the Indonesian exchange student Brian and I had hosted for six months the year before. We were due to leave on 18 August 1988, just ten weeks after Jim's death. Was this too soon? In July, I took Mim to Moonta for a weekend break where she mulled over the decision whether to go on the three-week trip. Stoically, she decided yes, she would.

From Darwin we flew to Denpasar, where Ica's father Salim met us at the steps of the plane, ushered us through customs as VIPs, had his staff collect our luggage, and installed us in our hotel. The next day, he flew with us to his home in Ujung Pandang, Sulawesi, fearfully praying all the way on the Garuda flight. He and his wife Sinta cared for Mum so warmly that she was able to relax, cry, and feel loved. Sinta spoke almost no English, but there was rich communication between them. Salim was Muslim and Sinta was Christian. The combination presented them with many holidays and celebrations which the whole family enjoyed.

After a few days relaxing with the family, Salim drove Mim and me to the far north of Sulawesi, to Tana Toraja, where the local people revere the dead so much that their effigies look out over the village keeping a close eye on the living. Instead of burying the dead, they keep the bones in wooden cradles in small caves in the cliff face. It was only on being invited to look in one of these caves that Mim was overcome. She could not face those dry old bones. Too much death.

Back in the beautiful wooden Dutch colonial guest house, she sobbed. Salim proffered a neck massage, which brought her back to the present when it became a little too intimate for comfort! From then on she was strong, interested and keen for new experiences, astounding the Indonesian family with her independence and resilience. They were amazed that she managed her own money and that I treated her with respect – Westerners were known for not respecting their elders!

Before heading home, we spent a few nights in what Ica had boasted was his uncle's 'big hotel' in Kuta, Bali. The 'hotel' turned out to be a poor losmen, cheap accommodation with few facilities, such as only one sheet on each hard bed. We had to learn the Indonesian word for towel in order to get one, but we enjoyed delicious banana fritters for breakfast made by the two young staff with no English.

The holiday ended in Kakadu, after we'd recovered from the culture shock of seeing Darwin's drab empty streets compared with Denpasar's colourful, crowded, chaotic roads.

Back home, Mim picked up her active social life, staying with friends, going to lunch with the Probus club, WD & HO Wills – her first annual lunch there as a widow – and the Arts Society, in the lead-up to Christmas. The worst moment came at the doleful Christmas dinner at home with Brian and me and the children. She didn't feel like celebrating Christmas without Dad, but we couldn't let her spend it alone. Before I served the traditional plum pudding that she had prepared, however, she suddenly stood up and almost ran next door to have a drink with our neighbours, Jill and Rod Heal. The diary fairly shouts, '25 Dec Chris and Brian for Xmas dinner. Jill and Rod!!' Sally followed Mim and joined the Heals for drinks until merriment took over and we all arrived and joined in.

Jim's death had a profound effect on Mim and Judy. The following April, Mim had an ultrasound and brain scan for unspecified health problems. At the same time, Judy began to act strangely, bringing in the washing when it was wet, and wandering about lost while going to the local shops. She was increasingly anxious and paranoid so the local GP put her on a psychotic drug without planning any follow-up. To family and friends, his approach seemed far too casual, and we urged Mim to get specialist advice. But Mim wouldn't take further action. Alarmed, Rob and Janet took Judy to an after-hours clinic where she was referred to Fullarton Private Hospital on 29 April 1989. Mim was furious with this family interference, compromising her trust in us. Over the next three months that Judy was in hospital, we all supported Mim in her daily visits to the hospital.

Judy descended rapidly into withdrawal and hallucination as, one after the other, three medications failed to stabilise her. She was in hospital when Mim's diary entry of 14 June notes, 'Judy found. Police.' I wanted a second opinion as it seemed the psychiatrist had no idea of her normal capacity. I discussed what was happening with a psychiatrist friend at Pilgrim Church, who said he was willing to see her. Mim agreed. She was as worried, as I was, that Judy was getting so much worse. But the hospital psychiatrist was furious when Mim suggested a second opinion, and especially angry that I had already spoken to another professional behind his back. His anger provoked Mim to say it was all my idea, not hers, and not what she wanted! Now Mim was furious with me, and siding with the psychiatrist. The next day, I came out in a severe rash that persisted for months.

A few weeks later, on a new medication, Judy improved suddenly, and was allowed to come home for an afternoon once a week, before being discharged on 1 September. Her sudden recovery made me realise that no matter what I did, Judy's well-being had nothing to do with me. Until that time, I had felt responsible for her, trying to make up for the pluses in my life that were minuses in hers. It was a revelation to realise that I could not change her life.

In the years following Jim's death, the co-dependence and the clashes between Mim and Judy intensified. When I visited or took them out, they both competed for my attention, both wanted to talk and complain, and neither listened to the other. Mim confided that I was her best friend, but it didn't feel like that to me. For years there had been so much I thought we couldn't talk about for all the differences in our opinions, and I often felt that she judged me.

Mim was a very harsh critic of herself, just as she herself had been so harshly criticised in her childhood and youth. She applied a high level of judgement to others, particularly women, and especially to her daughters-in-law. She thought I bent over backwards to understand other people and to rationalise their behaviour, while I thought this was a direct product of my upbringing with Judy. I always had to listen carefully to understand what Judy was saying. Mixing with people with disability prepared me to observe others closely for their level of understanding and their responses. These skills were fundamental to my work in adult literacy.

Although Mim had many friends, I think her self-judgement, the loss of her mother, and the abuse from her step-grandmother prevented her from closely trusting and confiding in women. She was more comfortable with men, but she rarely shared her very private feelings. Perhaps she shared them with Jim in later years during those long evening chats when they became friends, free of the stresses and hardships of the earlier years of their marriage.

Indonesian boarders

In the 1980s, Tricia and Stephen expanded the family's cross-cultural experiences through their American Field Service (AFS) student exchanges, Trish to Sabah in 1986 and Steve to Argentina in 1989. While they were overseas, their bedrooms at home were soon occupied by AFS students coming to Adelaide. In 1987 Yin Tje-ting, a teacher from China, stayed for six months and was later joined by Ica from Sulawesi, also with us for six months. As soon as Steve went away, we were pressed to take in an Indonesian student. Djoko was doing a Masters degree at Flinders University. He was a mature-age, high-ranking civil servant from Java with impeccable manners, and he called me Mrs Christ. He loved talking to Mim, who became 'Mum' to him over many long chats in the fading light of the early evenings. Djoko had left behind a wife and two teenage daughters and was homesick, and struggling with the Australian diet, culture and language. In his

Chris, Djoko's wife Mien, Rob, Mim, Djoko and friend with son.

Djoko with Mim at her birthday dinner, 1989.

grief, he couldn't be seen to cry, but he sniffed a lot when he was sad. Within two weeks of coming to stay with us, Djoko brought home a fellow student, Sitohang, to see if he could also board with us. We already had Brian's niece, Jenny, living with us, and there was no spare room. Until we could find a place for him, he shared a room with Djoko. I hoped that Mim would consider having an Indonesian boarder and was thrilled that she was open to the suggestion.

On 10 March 1989, Sitohang went to stay with Mim. He was the first of her many boarders, most from Indonesia, some from China, one Australian, some from other Asian countries. Many of these students became her friends, sharing confidences, bringing their families to visit, and she in turn visited some of them in Indonesia.

While Judy was in hospital, a new Indonesian boarder, Henys, had moved in to Mim's house. He was a fellow student of Djoko's, also studying for a Masters degree in Population Studies at Flinders. In contrast to Djoko's suave, Javanese, Muslim urbanity, Henys was from northern Sumatra, swarthy, loud, a Christian and depressed. He soon became part of the family. Several Indonesians now visited Mim regularly, including Sitohang and his family and friends. When Judy went for a holiday at Minlaton, Djoko and Henys drove Mim there to pick her up.

Mim was seventy-eight when I dropped the bombshell that I was separating from Brian and would be moving out of Carlisle Road after Christmas – another miserable Christmas for all of us. Mim's sympathies lay with Brian and with Steve, who was about to return from his AFS year in Argentina and was not yet aware of his parents' drama. Neither was Djoko aware of the impending separation, despite living with us. Shortly after my departure in January, Djoko moved in with Mim, so she now had two boarders, one in the sunroom and one in my old bedroom. Many evenings were spent chatting with both of them in the fading light, until Djoko's return to Jakarta in early 1992. A postcard from New York in 1993 is addressed 'For: My Mum Ingleton' and closes, 'See you again Mum'. We did not see him again as he died a premature death from hepatitis.

With my divorce a year later, Mim must have contemplated the disappointment of all her three children being divorced, Rob and Pat in 1979, Judy and Michael in 1984, Brian and me in 1989. This 'unfamily' tree extends back to her grandfather and forward into her grandchildren's generation.

Now another separation was about to happen: Judy wanted to move out. She was unhappy with her role of cleaner and shopper, physically tired from the work and miserable with her life at Hawthorn. She wanted to be independent again. Mim, however, had had enough of supporting Judy's moves – to Balyana, to Novar Gardens and to the granny flat. Each exacted the physical and emotional toll of preparation and mopping up, and she couldn't face another change.

Rob and I felt it was now our responsibility to find an answer to the question of 'what next?' Jim had charged Rob to look after Judy when he was gone, and I still had a strong sense of responsibility. With both Mim and Judy so miserable, something had to be done, and we felt we had to do it against Mim's wishes. In early 1991, Judy and I drove around at weekends looking at flats and units, without saying much to Mim, to see if it was realistic financially and practically for Judy to be able to live independently. A solution emerged. Janet knew of an independent living unit previously used by staff at Oxford Eldercare, Hove, in close proximity to Rob and me. Rob could ferry Judy to Mim's once a week to clean and shop.

Judy was thrilled. Mim was devastated. She was angry that we had undermined her yet again and further lost her trust in us. In some instances, she tried to drive a wedge between Rob and me, but thankfully Janet made sure we communicated more closely before damage was done. On 24 August 1991, Judy moved to Hove and managed her independence well. The arrangement did not improve their relationship, though, as Mim was dissatisfied and needed more help than she was now getting. Judy's cleaning and shopping for Mim on Fridays exhausted her, and by the end of the day words between them were sharp. Fridays became a day of dread for Rob, facing two cranky women and listening to complaints all the way home.

A happier outcome of Judy's move was that the granny flat was now available for a series of uni students who provided warm company, were in need of English conversation and watched out for Mim. She was pleased to preside over a liaison between two of these students, Ming from China and Ina from Indonesia, who married in August 1993.

Eighty plus

Mim wanted to do something adventurous on her eightieth birthday in November 1991. She was thrilled to go out with Sally, her boyfriend and some mates for a day's fishing a few kilometres off Glenelg. They were under strict instructions to have Mim home by four p.m. By then, Rob would have put up a huge banner saying, 'Happy 80th Birthday Mim!' and fifty unexpected guests would have arrived. All was in place, cars had been surreptitiously parked, and a sense of expectation filled the lounge and dining room. Time passed. And passed. Where were they? By four-thirty, excitement had dropped to low murmurs; by five, general conversation took up the space between bewilderment and worry.

Suddenly the trio burst in to the kitchen, Sally, her boyfriend and Mim, laughing and relaxed. Mim was in her fishing clothes and flat

Mim's eightieth birthday.

shoes, her hair wild. Coming from the kitchen into the lounge, she froze. All these people! And she looked a wreck! As Sally confided much later, she was also just a bit tiddly. They had had a marvellous adventure and downed plenty of stubbies. Time had become elastic, and way out to sea it was late before anyone thought to check the time. Now the party came to life and it was a great celebration. Mim never forgot coming to her own party in fishing clothes. She was a stickler

Four generations, 1993. Stevie, Sally, Chris, Mim.

for dressing smartly in long shirts and pants to conceal her thin limbs, and never left the house without heels, even to visit the neighbours.

One night in December 1996, on her way to the bathroom, Mim fell in the passage and could not get up. She thought her hip had broken, causing the fall. It took her eight hours to inch along the passage and finally reach the kitchen. The phone was out of reach on the kitchen bench but luckily the cord was hanging down. Mim pulled on the cord till the phone crashed to the floor. She dialled 000. When the ambulance arrived, the medics couldn't get in so they rang Rob. He sped along Daws Road at ninety kilometres an hour, the scariest drive of his life, and broke in through her bedroom window. Neither of the family's security plans had worked. Mim had moved the hidden key in case somebody found it, and her medi-alert was safely under her pillow, where she always left it. All did not go smoothly at Ashford either, where she fell out of bed not long after her hip operation.

Mim was now eighty-five. She was the lightest adult the surgeon had ever operated on, standing at one hundred and forty-seven centimetres and weighing in at thirty-seven kilos. Her new artificial joint could be seen below the skin as there was no fat to conceal it. The surgeon said the broken hip was the beginning of the 'slippery slope'

Judy and Mim, 1993.

to dependence and that we should be prepared. Just before Christmas, Mim left Ashford and went to Griffith Hospital for rehabilitation for six weeks. Now the question was, how would she manage at home?

Mim was adamant she would not go into care, but we were able to convince her that some respite care would be beneficial. She agreed and spent two weeks in Sturt Palms at Brighton, close to all her children. However, the condescending, overly cheerful morning call of 'Rise and shine, pets!' grated badly, along with the insistence on having to get up for breakfast by a particular time. She was never going there again!

Back home, she felt secure in her daily routine with the familiarity of the home she'd lived in for nearly forty years, and she did not plan to leave it. Despite her badly declining eyesight due to macular degeneration, her osteoporosis and shortness of breath, she was determined to look after herself, continuing to potter in the garden, sweep the garden paths and prepare simple meals. Sometimes out driving we looked at possible accommodation for downsizing, but she damned modern places as 'little boxes'. They were certainly not for her.

The local GP, Dr Anderson, became a frequent visitor on his way home from the clinic around the corner, unwinding in the peaceful late

Mim in her garden with Maya and Trish, 1994.

afternoon chats he enjoyed with Mim in the sunroom, and meeting various family members as we called in after work. More and more frequently, we arrived to see her using the nebuliser to cope with her chronic obstructive pulmonary disease. After the nebuliser, she'd light up and enjoy her favourite brand of cigarette. There were two reasons she refused to give up smoking: she didn't inhale, she said, and it was her only real pleasure – why stop at this age? On the contrary, one of her greatest pleasures was to sit and smoke with her grandchildren, Sally and Naomi, the only smokers left in the family. Dad had given up the habit in his sixties after a severe bout of bronchitis and Rob had recently given up to save his blood pressure.

These were the pleasures she enjoyed most now. But she regretted that she was no longer 'useful'. Because she measured her usefulness by what she could do for others, she felt her life no longer had purpose. Her neighbours, the Brockies across the road, had said to her in their eighties, 'Mu, old age is not for the faint-hearted.' With her stoicism, Mim was not faint-hearted; it was the feeling of uselessness that depleted her now. There was little she could do for her family, though at eighty-four she delighted in arranging a Cousins' Day to bring together most of her extending family. (She also exerted her power by excluding Janet from the gathering on the grounds it was for Rob's children not hers!)

Cousins' Day, 1995.

Mim and Angie.

In mid-1997 and again in mid-1998 Mim agreed to two weeks' respite care at Alwyndor Aged Care facility at Hove. This venue was far more successful. She found a smoking partner she enjoyed talking to on a sheltered veranda, and she could have breakfast in her room at any time.

The following February, however, Mim was depressed. Steve and Angie's wedding was to be celebrated on the beach at Port Noarlunga. From the top of the cliffs, she had to be pushed in a wheelchair down the steep, rocky path of the cliff face and through the soft sand to the water's edge. She hated being seen in a wheelchair. At the reception at Angie's parents' home, Mim appeared to be overcome by the sure knowledge she would not be with her growing family much longer. Sally can't forget the grief and foreknowledge in her eyes that evening.

Just a few weeks later, the onset of extreme abdominal pain meant a stay in St Andrew's Hospital for two weeks with no clear diagnosis. From there, she went to Glenelg Private Hospital to recover, eat well and build her strength. A second, more severe attack, saw her back at St Andrews in a week. When asked in Emergency where she rated her pain on a scale of one to ten, she simply said 'Eleven'. By the time X-rays revealed a blockage in the bowel, she was unconscious.

Steve and Mim.

Two young interns had a quiet chat with me. 'The surgeons will want to operate, but our advice would be, don't let them. The anaesthetic alone, let alone the operation, would be too much for her.'

When Mim woke up, she was cheered to see so many members of the family around her. She was chatting when the surgeon arrived to present a choice: would she consent to an operation or not?

'What do you think?' she asked me.

'I would advise No,' I said, giving the interns' reasons.

Mim considered this for no more than five seconds then said firmly, 'Yes, I'll have it! Please ring Naomi [Janet's daughter] and tell her to come in before I go into theatre.'

We didn't know that was code for 'I'm going to die, and I want to say goodbye to you.' Only Naomi knew the code. By the time she arrived, however, Mim had already gone into theatre.

Mim survived the operation. A week later, she sat up and asked for her bright red lipstick to make herself presentable to staff and visitors. But her burst of energy was short-lived. A few days later, after a discussion with her doctor, I told her that there would be no further treatment and the morphine would be increased to keep her comfortable and make her sleep. I didn't know how to say 'until the end' and she looked at me sharply. I wish I could have used Trish's words to me in a recent birthday card, 'Thank you, Mum, for guiding us with your wisdom And opening our minds to the world.'

Mim's hospital room had a view over the tall eucalypts in the parklands and across to the Adelaide Hills. She enjoyed this view, as she had always enjoyed nature. Mim fixed her gaze on her last sight of nature as daylight waned. Trish stayed the night with her as she slept until passing away peacefully in the early morning of 22 April 1999.

10

Searching for Mim's Father

Five years later, Judy and I took the train to Broken Hill for a week's holiday. I visited the Broken Hill Family History Group in the Trades Hall, Blende Street, to find information about my grandmother.

Jenny Camilleri was on duty that day, 27 May 2004. 'Can I help you?' she asked.

'I'm looking for information about my grandmother, Isobel Muriel Read. She had an illegitimate daughter, Henrietta Muriel, who was born on 9 November 1911 in Broken Hill,' I replied.

'I think I know something about that!' Jenny said, stepping towards an old grey filing cabinet. She hunted through the files. 'Yes, here's a card,' and she passed me a handwritten card:

> HENRIETTA M READ   1911   BH   1/11/05 Samuel Sanderson's child?
>   ISABEL M Read   (38210)   age 22
>
> ISABELL M Read (m) 1912   Henry   age 23
>   FRANKLIN — 13405
>
>   Isabella Muriel Franklin died Bungle &c
>   28·12·1915
>   age 26   26
>   brother   1889
>   A. W. Read
>
> HUS. Henry FRANKLIN DIED 12·10·1934 age 54
> Mrs F.S Bennetts Adelaide - GAWLER - SISTER
> Miss Eileen Franklin
>
>   Maybe the illg child of Samuel Seymour
>   Sanderson

'Perhaps you want to sit down,' she offered, seeing my shocked face. 'Actually, I wrote that several years ago. I was recording an oral history with my great-aunt, in her eighties, the last survivor of my grandparents' generation. She told me that her brother, Samuel Seymour Sanderson, had once confided that when he was engaged to be married to my mother Ruby, he got another young woman pregnant, and I believe that it was Isobel Read, who had lived nearby. He never told anyone else. That was when I added this note to the file. It is still a question mark, but I'm pretty sure it's true. If it is, that means you and I are cousins!'

That was a lot to take in!

The following day, Judy and I met Jenny and her two sisters, exclaimed over similarities in hair and skin colouring and body shape, and wondered at this very surprising turn of events. Was it true? Was

Samuel Sanderson with daughter Ruby – Henrietta Muriel Read's father and half-sister?

Judy with the Broken Hill grandchildren of Samuel Sanderson – our cousins? May 2004.

there a resemblance? Jenny gave us photocopies of Samuel Sanderson with baby Ruby Jean – Mim's half-sister, and his wife Clara (née Palin). The Sanderson Family Record Sheet shows that Samuel and Clara were married on 7 September 1910 and Ruby was born on 10 February 1911. Samuel not only got Clara pregnant out of wedlock, but went on to get Isobel pregnant with Muriel just after he was married! Jenny Camilleri's mother was that baby Ruby, while my mother was that baby Muriel. Another part of the unfamily tree!

A convict history

I was curious about Samuel, my newly acquired grandfather. What was he like? Where did he come from? Living in Broken Hill, he worked at BHP as a mill-hand. His father George, although born in Tasmania, also worked at BHP, as a foreman. Samuel's grandfather, John Sanderson, was born in Yorkshire in 1807, arriving in Port Jackson on the ship *Lady Nugent*, not as a free settler or a soldier, but as a convict.

John Sanderson was an illiterate coal miner, short and tattooed. I'm reluctant to write that one of his tattoos read,

> love and unity
> pretty girl good opportunity
> a dark room a feather bed
> her maiden head

John was aged about twenty-seven when he was convicted for highway robbery and sentenced to life imprisonment. Jenny Camilleri shared an identikit image of John, and information from his convict records.

John Sanderson
Standing Number 35–1051; Indent Number: 94
Extract from Sydney Convict Records 35/1

Education: none
Religion: Church of England
Marital status: married
Children: none
Native place: Yorkshire: Hull
Trade or calling: coal miner
Tried at Lancaster Assizes, UK, 3 March 1834. Former conviction of 6 months.
Sentenced to life imprisonment for highway robbery.
Transported to Sydney 3 December 1834 aboard the *Lady Nugent* with 285 convicts.
Arrived in Sydney, New South Wales, 3 August 1835.

27 September 1836	25 lashes: making away with his rations
25 October 1836	50 lashes: disobedience of orders
4 April 1837	50 lashes: absconding
2 October 1838	7 days cells: disorderly conduct

Tried at Maitland Quarter Sessions 23 November 1841 for Burglary. Sentenced to 15 years in Port Arthur.

8 July 1842	7 days cells: fighting

Sent to Hobart on 23 June 1843 on the ship *Sir John Byng* with 33 convicts, arriving one week later.

22 February 1844	Reprimanded: neglect of work
27 May 1844	Reprimanded: misconduct
9 October 1844	6 days solitary confinement: misconduct
7 January 1845	10 days solitary confinement: contrary to orders
30 June 1846	Solitary confinement: misconduct
22 September 1848	Reprimanded: coalmine: gambling:
17 October 1848	Ticket of Leave
17 March 1849	1 month hard labour: not reporting his arrival in district

10 December 1849	Drinking: discharged
25 December 1851	Recommended for Conditional Pardon
16 March 1852	Absent from Muster
20 January 1853	3 months hard labour: out after hours
26 July 1853	Conditional Pardon approved

John Sanderson gained his pardon nearly twenty years after his transportation. His first child, also John, was born soon after in Tasmania on 7 September 1854, to Sarah Harris, a nurse. They married the following year in Newcastle, NSW, and George was born on 27 March at Douglas River, back in Tasmania.

How ironic that one great-great-grandfather was a police inspector while the other has made a late appearance as a convict, and a very troublesome one at that!

The telling of Mim's story begins with a storm of curses and ends with the solution to a mystery. Despite her infamous grandmother, the shame of her illegitimacy, losing her mother at four, being brought up by a harsh step-grandmother, and never knowing who her father was, Mim was strong and resilient. She developed a capacity to love and be loved that was a rich gift to her family, her friends and her community.

www.ingramcontent.com/pod-product-compliance
Lightning Source LLC
Chambersburg PA
CBHW070926080526
44589CB00013B/1442